Mornings *With* OSWALD

Daily Reflections With My Utmost For His Highest

Dr. Donald M. Minter

xulon
PRESS

Copyright © 2014 by Dr. Donald M. Minter

Mornings With Oswald
Daily Reflections With My Utmost For His Highest
by Dr. Donald M. Minter
Cover image provided by Dr. Thomas Jay Oord

Printed in the United States of America

ISBN 9781498412308

Scripture quotations are taken from the New International Version (NIV). Copyright © 1973, 1978, 1984, 2011 by Biblica, Inc.™. Used by permission. All rights reserved.

www.xulonpress.com

INTRODUCTION

A Moment On Method:

I first began meeting with Oswald Chambers in the early 1980s after strong encouragement from another friend. So Oswald and I began our morning chats, like all new acquaintances, cautiously and carefully. I soon realized I had stumbled onto a friend who would journey with me for the remainder of my life, which, of course, is a bit odd considering the fact he died in 1917, nearly 65 years before our first conversation. His book, My Utmost For His Highest, quickly became a guide for my journey, and countless others, into the Kingdom of God. Soon, he and I were regulars at the table with the King.

This gathering of friends is the oldest of the 'spiritual disciplines', an early daily encounter with God's Word, setting the stage for the complexity of life in the day ahead. This encounter, like all good relationships, ought not be rushed; instead, a time of leisure for old friends to chat, reflecting on life with all of its twists and nuances. Oswald and I will grab a seat next to you, so grab a cup of your favorite elixir, settle down and enjoy your daily conversation with old and new friends. Be warned, another friend, the Holy Spirit, has been known to pop in on occasion to join the conversation. When He does no telling what lies ahead. He has been known to be unruly and unpredictable. Oswald and I both will attest to that. Don't sweat it, it's just His way, so relax and enjoy the dialogue. You will quickly discover, He, more times than not, has something to say.

In the end, only those who learn to 'apply' the conversation to everyday living will return to this daily meeting of the minds. Application, unique and personal, generating a lust for more, a lust that can never be satisfied, is the key to feasting at this daily table. Fear not, application is always custom built. The Spirit has this way of providing particulars with only you in mind.

A final warning for those who choose to journey on. The road could get bumpy, perhaps even impassable, at times. Once unleashed, the Serving King rarely chooses an autobahn for cruising down life's highway. But keep the peddle to the metal. He is taking you places you have never dared to imagine. When you get there, the few, the saints from earlier conversations, will be waiting. And what a glorious time of storytelling will begin...

Trek on...

ACKNOWLEDGEMENTS

I began this project in the early days of personal computers. Unfortunately, like so many others, much of it was lost in the great computer failure of 1997 (who knew computers died). So my daily conversations with Oswald went unrecorded in the mystical land of digitized data. But, my bride (Laura DaForno Minter) encouraged me to reengage, and the rest is history. I have loved her more with each passing day. Without her and her amazing editorial skills, this project would still be in the never-never land of digitized burial grounds. A better companion no man has ever known.

In 2013, my mother and father (S. Wayne Minter and Ramona Minter), faithful readers of whatever I write, good or bad, insisted I make the book available to more than just those 'trekking' along with me via social media. Their blind optimism made this project possible. And no, this project is not nearly as good as they think. Life doesn't get any better than being loved for a lifetime by your mom and dad.

However, ultimately, I wrote this book for my boys (Dustin, Derek and Michael). I wanted to leave them with the opportunity to chat with me long after my days of preoccupation on this spinning ball are over (forgive me boys). But I'm hoping the conversations will begin long before the clock strikes midnight.

And, of course, for all of you who waited patiently for each morning's dispatch, thank you! Not sure Oswald and I would have shown up each day had you not been faithfully waiting.

Trek on...

* A special thanks to Dr. Thomas Jay Oord in providing the amazing photographs.
* All Oswald Chamber quotes are taking from Chambers, O. (1986). My Utmost For His Highest: Selections For The Year. Grand Rapids, MI –Oswald Chambers Publications; Marshall Pickering.

Day 1
DO YOU KNOW?

I eagerly expect and hope that I will in no way be ashamed, but will have sufficient courage so that now as always Christ will be exalted in my body, whether by life or by death.
(Philippians 1:20)

"Paul is determined that nothing shall deter him from doing exactly what God wants." – Oswald Chambers

Therein lies the great battle for moderns, "Knowing exactly what it is God wants." It is the modern dilemma, the great frustration, the limiting factor of a life well spent, the 'grand disabler of the 21st century': We just don't seem to know what God wants. Then the suggestion no one wants to admit: God generates that awful, life-changing 'providential crisis', an unavoidable moment where the 'want of God' cannot be missed. God's will is known. The simplicity of that startling moment, a moment in which the 'want of God' is so abundantly clear, our old friend, our comforting and disabling companion, 'I don't know what God wants', flees out the window, leaving us a stark new reality, a moment of clarity in which the 'want of God' shines so brightly it simply cannot be missed. Ignorance, our old cherished friend, gone.

Then, nowhere to run, nowhere to hide, no excuse to claim, no beloved 'ignorance to hide in', we simply must decide, "Do I have the courage to exalt Christ in the particular this or that before me?" As Paul so rightly knows, all we can do is 'eagerly expect' and 'hope' we will stand tall in the 'moment of clarity'. There is much more 'clarity' to come for those who refuse to be 'ashamed', who actualize the clarity of 'God wants' into a moment of profound and simple obedience, who dare to trek on.

So the discovery of the lifelong trek after the Serving King and the trauma of recognition, a lifetime of moment-by-moment decisions lay ahead. And the reasonable doubt begins to arise, "Will I have sufficient courage to be and do what God makes 'known' concerning my life?" Then comes the moment of courage to 'be and do' as God has directed, in this moment, for this day. Trek after the Serving King, one day at time, with just enough insight and courage for today. Tomorrow will have enough trouble of its own. There is much more clarity to come. Trek on in today's moment of clarity.

Day 2
GPS CERTAINTY

**...even though he did not know where he was going.
(Hebrews 11:8)**

"One of the difficulties in Christian work is this question–'What do you expect to do?' You do not know what you are going to do; the only thing you know is that God knows what He is doing... It is this attitude that keeps you in perpetual wonder– you do not know what God is going to do next."– Oswald Chambers

More times than not in the moment of 'clarity', that moment when you finally 'know' what it is God desires of you, a realization surfaces with great cause for alarm, "I have no idea what the consequences of this will be, no insight into what will come next, or where this will lead." Such was the trauma for Abraham, hearing ever so clearly from God, direction for the 'moment', and only that moment. How contrary to our world of 'GPS' certainty, street-by-street clarity, turn-by-turn assurance, until arriving at your predetermined destiny with speed and ease.

Trekking with God offers no such certainty, no 'expect this or that' after 'turning this way or that'. No, God rarely provides GPS instruction and precision beyond the 'immediate moment'. Instead, God simply calls, "Follow closely" as God leads in the certainty of the 'present moment' and little more. The promise of a 'well-intentioned' destination is always before you, but you will rarely get to see it until your arrival. Be not surprised along the way as you "live in tents with Isaac and Jacob, heirs with him of the same promise...looking forward to the city that has foundations, whose Designer and Builder is God" (Hebrews 11:10).

Can you really learn to follow God in the certainty of the moment as God leads? Or will you always need to ask, "Where are we going?" Those needing GPS certainty are not well suited for a journey of 'moment by moment' trekking after God. So a decision must be made to follow closely behind God into the unknowns of tomorrow. It is often a lonely journey into the land of the unknown. Can you find the courage to walk into unknown as you trek after the God Who leads? Trek on...

Day 3
THE VOICE IN THE DARKNESS

...clouds and thick darkness surround Him.
(Psalm 97:2)

"The only possibility of understanding the teaching of Jesus is by the light of the Spirit of God on the inside."– Oswald Chambers

Access to God, for the novice, often seems so simple, "Jesus loves me this I know." In some sense, it is as simple as "Jesus loves me." But for those seeking to 'know' God, to experience the intimacy of 'knowing' God, to dive deep into the very being of God, the journey through the 'clouds and darkness' can be debilitating in the worst possible way. You are not well suited for long periods of 'clouds and darkness', especially with so many scary sounds and noises rushing at you from the dark. So you will be tempted to run back into the light, the simpler way of trekking after God, the elementary insights into God, the safety of what so many 'know' of God, of what 'others' have heard from God. The crowd offers great comfort to the novice.

However, for those willing to stay in the 'clouds and thick darkness', those who remain steadfast in the 'last known direction from God', a ray of light, a brilliant moment of insight, a 'revelation', flashes into sight. This deeper seeing is never seen with the 'eyes', rather it is simply 'known'. It is the 'wisdom of God' only found in the light of the 'Spirit of the Living God', as the Spirit whispers insight into the mind of the follower standing in the 'clouds and thick darkness'. It will often not be seen by another, one who can validate the message of the whispering Spirit; rather, it is mediated directly by the Spirit, in the ear of one standing in the 'clouds and thick darkness', in the very presence of the Living God.

Not all who have been called will be able to tread along into the heart and mind of God. But some will. They will gather in the 'clouds and thick darkness', surprised by the presence of another trekking after the King.

Day 4

YOU CAN'T GO

**Peter asked, "Lord, why can't I follow You now?"
(John 13:37)**

"Natural devotion may be all very well to attract us to Jesus, to make us feel His fascination, but it will never make us disciples. Natural devotion will always deny Jesus somewhere or other." – Oswald Chambers

It is nothing new for the child of God to desire constant fellowship. No child responds well to being released from the safety and warmth of mother, especially if mother's intention for the 'child left behind' is to 'love' the remaining siblings. What a profound 'change of purpose' is ushered in with the departure of mother! The abandoned child goes from being 'nurtured' to nurturer. For some children, children like Peter, this will be more than they can bear to carry. Peter quickly responds to the command, "As I have loved you, you must love one another..." with a passionate plea to continue trekking alongside Jesus, freed from the burden of the 'others'. Oh the joy of remaining in the presence of Christ Jesus.

'Loving as Jesus loved' is quite simply the 'essence' of the Christian experience, and it is inevitably costly, more costly than anyone could anticipate. The transition from 'recipient' of love to 'giver' of love is tantamount to 'losing one's life' for the sake of others. Hence, you will be tempted to say with Peter, "Lord, why can't I follow You now?" And He will say, "Because you are not yet ready to 'lay down your life for Me', to love those whom I love, those whom will not love you back in the way that you need to be loved, those whom will abuse you when you love them." So for now, simply "love one another," your brothers and sisters, those who will love you back. And yes, even that will be much harder than you have imagined.

But be of good cheer. A time will come, perhaps a time much sooner than you expect, when following Jesus will present itself again, for the rooster crows for us all. Until that moment, rest in the comfort of your family and learn the basics of love. Trek on.

Day 5
I CAN'T DO THAT

**Jesus replied, "Where I am going, you cannot follow now,
but you will follow later."
(John 13:38)**

*"No matter what changes God has wrought in you, never rely
upon them, build only on a Person, the Lord Jesus Christ,
and on the Spirit He gives."– Oswald Chambers*

Early on, following Jesus seems 'doable', just a matter of 'deciding' to trek along after Him; especially in light of His orientation toward you and your every concern. There is great comfort in trekking with the Serving King, His attention seemingly on your every concern. But that changes in a radical manner, often unexpectedly. Eventually, you receive your first 'undoable' command creating a needed crisis, a watershed moment, opening the door for a major transformation in your 'being and doing'.

You will typically 'see it' long before the actual arrival at the 'moment of undoability'. You will marvel at how easy it seems for others to simply 'do it', to follow without hesitation in the moment of their 'later' suddenly arriving. In that moment, you are left wondering, "How do they do that? How do they 'do' what seems so incredibly 'undoable'?" You will be tempted to say, "They are more experienced, more practiced and with experience and practice must come a 'doability' that to date eludes me." There may be some truth found here, but the 'following later' of which Jesus speaks is not simply a matter of experience and practice. No, this 'following later' requires a 'potency' that experience and practice cannot provide. Something far richer is required.

Much of what Jesus will require of you 'later' in your trekking after Him can only be accomplished in the 'presence and power' of the Holy Spirit. That rarely comes easy for those so empowered, knowing failure awaits unless the Spirit manifests repeatedly. And yes, there is always a new "you cannot follow now, but you will follow later." Such is the life of continual transformation in this quest after Jesus. The journey never ends and with each new surroundings comes new challenges for all those intent on trekking on.

Day 6
SOMEWHERE IN THE MIDDLE

**From there he went on toward the hills east of Bethel and pitched his tent, with Bethel on the west and Ai on the east. There he built an altar to the Lord and called on the name of the Lord.
(Genesis 12:8)**

"Bethel is the symbol of communion with God; Ai is the symbol of the world. Abraham pitched his tent between the two."– Oswald Chambers

It is what it is, a temporary station, a resting place in the trek after the Serving King, somewhere between solitude with God and that process of life called the 'rat race'. This is a mystical place where we 'pitch a tent', crawl inside, and 'call on God'. Few ever find this place in the midst of the daily grind, or better yet, 'build' this place to commune with God. Building takes time and energy, precious commodities for those in the 'rat race', but essential for those who are intent on doing more than just 'racing', who intend to actually win. The art of 'building' that place of solitude with God is the critical step so often missed by those 'racing along' at breakneck speeds, mandated by the world we live in.

But winning, not to be confused with simply 'racing', requires 'wisdom', knowing how and where to race, and wisdom comes from hearing God in the midst of a life flying by. Understand, hearing God in the midst of the 'rat race' is a learned skill, honed by practice and application, but what is more important is finding or building that 'place' where God can be found, or, more importantly, 'heard'. Hearing is the critical first step toward 'doing' as God would do. Hearing happens first in the 'tent', and only later in the actual 'rat race'. A hard lesson to learn.

Moderns seem to have mastered Bethel (church) and Ai (world), but struggle to build that 'tent' between the two, the very essence of 'incarnation', walking in this world while staying radically connected to the Father. Start by finding a moment, just a moment, to pause and pitch your 'tent' each day, this place between God and World, listening carefully for God's voice whispering in the 'moment of the tent'. Learn to listen carefully for just a 'moment', evermore carefully with each passing day, for this 'race' gets harder and harder, faster and faster. And yes, you are meant to do so much more than simply race. You are meant to win. Trek on...

Day 7
TODAY'S INTIMACY

"Don't you know Me, Philip, even after I have been among you such a long time?"
(John 14:9)

"It was a wonderful intimacy, but there was a much closer intimacy to come..."– Oswald Chambers

It always startles us when someone we 'think' we know well, so well we have committed to trekking after Him, proclaims, "You still don't know me even after all these years?" And no, years of 'trekking' will not, by proximity, create this 'knowing Him'. Jesus may not rebuke us for our lack of 'knowing', still it surprises us, this frank honesty concerning our lack of 'knowing'.

It is a fundamental question you will need to ask on a consistent basis, "Do I know Him, really know Him, in the way He desires to be known?" The answer, of course, even after 'such a long time', is simply and always, "There is so much more yet to know." So the secret to a lifelong relationship, steeped in the depth of a relationship in which 'so much' is already known, and yet, 'so much more' still left to discover for those willing to look ever deeper.

Here is the rub, this 'yet to be known' can only be discovered through an 'intimacy' that has yet to be explored, yet to be 'experienced', yet to be entered into. This 'intimacy' is not offered to everyone; instead, only to those who have 'experienced' and 'embraced' prior moments of 'intimacy', unlocking the doorway to 'today's intimacy'. Be warned, what you discover and experience will not always please you, for Jesus rarely fits into our preconceived notions of 'Who' and 'What' He should be; instead, Jesus insists on transforming our 'notions', replacing them with an actual 'knowledge' of Who Jesus really is.

The 'many', fearing what is yet unknown, will cease to search for 'tomorrow's intimacy' with Him. The 'many' prefer the 'safe' and 'predictable' Jesus of yesterday. Only those who dare to evolve in their understanding of Jesus will come to 'know' Him in the intimacy of today's 'intimate moment'. Trek on...

Day 8

OUTRAGEOUS DEMANDS

**When they reached the place God had told him about, Abraham built an altar there and arranged the wood on it. He bound his son Isaac and laid him on the altar, on top of the wood.
(Genesis 22:9)**

"What God wants is the sacrifice through death which enables us..."– Oswald Chambers

It is easy to walk away from the radical demands of God early in the trek after the Serving King. Inexperience makes a quick turnaround easy, the way back home still within sight. But what about late in the journey, decades into the journey, deep enough into the journey that you have learned to trust God regardless of the 'outrageous' demands God may place upon you? For some, 'experience' will provide 'blind confidence' to whatever and whenever God calls. For others, though, 'experience' will provide little consolation, knowing God's ways are not our ways, and God's ways will call for action so improbable, actions having led others to the 'cross'.

No 'inside knowledge', a secret revelation things are not as they seem, is given concerning Abraham's obedience; rather, just that he was obedient. Thus, Abraham receives no hidden understanding of what is to come in the moments ahead. Isaac is bound and ready, as is Abraham. Father and son linked to a deadly game of obedience reserved only for the most faithful, those assured of 'direction' from God, undeniable 'clarity' of the worst kind.

Don't be surprised when 'late in the journey' God pushes and prods in ways that make you uncomfortable, right to edge, even crossing the 'line' at times. That is how God works in the lives of those who continue to trek after the Serving King. Nor expect comfort and ease in each and every moment of obedience. Such is not God's way. Sometimes it is the 'trembling hand' that offers the most profound moments of obedience before God.

Then comes the moment of stunning insight. Your faithfulness of 'trembling hand' pales in comparison to the faithfulness of the 'sacrificial lamb', the son, tied beneath the 'trembling hand'. And the thicket stirs. Father and son, theirs is the glory of obedience to 'outrageous demands'. Trek on...

Day 9
THE NEEDED FIX

May God Himself, the God of peace, sanctify you through and through. May your whole spirit, soul and body be kept blameless...
(I Thessalonians 5:23)

"Do we believe that God can garrison the imagination far beyond where we can go? 'The blood of Jesus Christ cleanseth us from all sin'– if that means in conscious experience only, may God have mercy on us."– Oswald Chambers

Youthfulness provides such innocence, an innocence wanting to believe in the inherent goodness of humanity, all of humanity, including 'self'. However, the journey, a journey all must take, slowly proves 'innocence' wrong, including a slow-to-die hopefulness in 'self'. Slowly comes the recognition 'self' cannot be fixed, nor cleansed, nor healed, nor improved, etc., by 'self'. As all discover eventually, 'self' is crippled, tainted, damaged ever so slightly or greatly, always enough to distort 'self' in a 'tragic' manner. A single 'degree' off course soon takes you miles from 'who' you intended to be. It is the great tragedy of the human condition.

As 'innocence' dies, so will hope, ultimately enabling you to accept the crippled 'self', even 'loving' the crippled 'self', perhaps even so bold as to declare the crippled 'self' good. However, those trekking after the Serving King discover a new source of 'hope', a source free of the limitations of 'self', free from the 'infection' of decay, free to 'be' and 'do' in ways that 'self' never could. God, discovered and embraced, set free to 'do' what only God can do with the damaged 'self'. The unthinkable now possible, healing for the crippled 'self', a new way of being and doing just over the horizon.

Be warned, God intends to 'fix' what really ails the 'self'. That 'fix' will probe and prod you to very core of your being into the 'whole spirit, soul and body'. As the Spirit of God bores into the very essence of your being, expect moments of discomfort, moments of 'self' discovery and cleansing, moments of anguish, moments of great joy, and, most profoundly, freedom for and from 'self'. A new way of 'being and doing' is ushered in, His way of 'being and doing'. Then, and only then, life authentically begins, liberated from the obsessions of the self-centered self. So we pray, "May the God of peace sanctify you through and through..." The trek is just beginning. Trek on...

17

Day 10
BREAKING THE CYCLE

"...to open their eyes and turn them from darkness to light, and from the power of Satan to God, so that they may receive forgiveness of sins and a place among those who are sanctified by faith in Me."
(Acts 26:18)

"Conversion is not regeneration. This is one of the neglected factors in our preaching today. When a man is born again, he knows that it is because he has received something as a gift from Almighty God and not because of his own decision."– Oswald Chambers

The gift of forgiveness is a glorious experience, but never intended to be a perpetual 'state of being', an ongoing condition, a mere cleansing of consequence, necessitated by continual failure in the same arenas, over and over again. Failure was never meant to be a condition for life, unredeemed by the 'gift' of forgiveness. No, Jesus poured out His life to overcome that vicious and crippling cycle of repetitive failure. Breaking 'the cycle' is the very point of His sending His Spirit to empower and overcome the 'power of Satan', even those long established 'strongholds' deep within the very fiber of who and what we are.

'Seeing' and consequent 'doing' are two very different entities. Seeing and understanding what God intends to do 'in' and 'with' you as God 'sanctifies' is one thing; but actualizing it, turning potential into reality, is quite another. That is the 'rub' that confounds. "Isn't God going to do all that needs to be done for me?"

When facing the 'undoable', what you cannot do, even under the empowering of the Holy Spirit, yes, God will certainly intercede for you. "All things are possible with God" (Matthew 19:26). So arises the ongoing temptation to proclaim, "I cannot do this!" But you are wrong. You can do this, better yet, "I can do all things through Him Who strengthens me..."(Philippians 4:13). So the 'power of Satan' is overcome, unleashing you to 'be and do' as does He who overcomes. However, you will have to 'turn from the darkness', the old ways of 'being and doing', and see the light. You have hidden far too long in the cries of "I can't do this." This is no longer about what you can do, rather what He can do in you. The time for new dreams has come. Trek on...

Day 11
THE HEAVIEST CROSS

As they led Him away, they seized Simon from Cyrene, who was on his way in from the country, and put the cross on him and made him carry it behind Jesus.
(Luke 23:26)

"If we are in love with our Lord, obedience does not cost us anything, it is a delight, but it costs those who do not love Him a good deal."– Oswald Chambers

Never confuse the 'delight' of relational obedience with the 'delight' of the specific task at hand. The latter will often not be 'delight' at all. Cross carrying is not, in and of itself, 'delightful'; to the contrary, 'cross carrying', without a relationship of obedience to the Christ, is unbearable. Be prepared for the reality that few carry the cross of Jesus alone. Instead, those you love, journeying with you, who trust you and depend on you, will often be the 'civilian casualties' in your trek after God.

Simon from Cyrene, an innocent bystander, soon finds himself in the middle of history's most profound moment, simply because he was watching the obedience of another. He was in the wrong place at the right time, or perhaps at the right place at the right moment, you decide. This is where you may stumble. Not when you are carrying your own cross, difficult as that will be, but rather, when those you care about, those you love, those you cannot bear to see suffer, have to suffer along with you, sometimes in ways worse than your own suffering.

You will have to get used to this 'suffering of others', if you are to survive this journey with Jesus, this trek after the Serving King. It is a continual pattern for those who follow Jesus, as others are 'caught in the wake' of your obedience. Nor does this pattern seem to dissipate with 'length of service' or even 'distance from a particular act of service'. The wake of your obedience can be long and wide. So be not surprised when 'they seize' the Simon of Cyrene in your life, family or friend, dragged into the consequences of your obedience, carrying the burden of the cross meant for you.

Can you continue trekking with Jesus as those around you are paying the cost of your obedience? You have discovered the heaviest cross of all, the cost to those whom you love and care for. This cross will not get lighter. Trek on...

19

Day 12

WHO AM I?

**But when He was alone with His Own disciples,
He explained everything.
(Mark 4:34)**

*"We have to get rid of the idea that we understand ourselves,
it is the last conceit to go." – Oswald Chambers*

Alone time, especially in this 'always connected' culture, is difficult, even when we desperately desire it. Harder yet is alone time with Jesus, those rare moments when you sense His presence, His very being, directly in front of you, eye-to-eye contact, that piercing presence of Jesus, exploring deep into the core of who you are. Rarer yet, that moment when Jesus explains to you what He sees, helps you comprehend the 'you' that He sees, the 'you' He hopes to transform, the 'you' that must understand what can only be understood with the eyes of Jesus, the voice of Jesus, leading you into an ever deeper self awareness.

Those moments will not occur often, so you must seize the moment when it arrives, learn all that you can learn in that moment of personal clarity. The conceit of 'positive self evaluation' will come crashing down in these moments. The infection of sin and self-absorbed self will flash before you in ways that will startle you as they violate your 'good' self-image, your 'better than most' secret evaluation. You will be tempted to pause there and mourn. However, 'insight' is not about 'self-pity' rather transformation and redemption, a healing more profound than you ever dared to imagine.

Thus, 'understanding' is not simply about seeing the problem, but, more importantly, fixing the problem. This 'explained everything' Jesus provides for those who dare to listen and learn, to stay in the conversation, is a 'comprehensive everything' that will show you both fault and provision for change. Of course, remaining to hear 'everything' will require time and courage. It is in these moments of 'personal clarity', His 'explained everything', that the trek after the Serving King takes on profound meaning and transformation. Dare to listen carefully. You are in the rarest of moments with the Serving King. Trek on...

Day 13
WHAT HAVE YOU ASKED?

**When He was alone, the Twelve and the others around
Him asked Him about the parables.
(Mark 4:10)**

*"If you are going on with God, the only thing that is clear to
you, and the only thing God intends to be clear, is the way He
deals with your own soul. Your brother's sorrows and perplexities are an absolute confusion to you." – Oswald Chambers*

Clarity regarding 'this' or 'that' inevitably leads to confusion in other
areas long ago 'settled' and 'stored away'. It is the natural consequence
of being taught by the Serving King. Thus, trekking with Jesus can be
uncomfortable, not just initially, but throughout the follower's lifetime. That
is why those who trek after Jesus will have to master the art of asking
questions, questions seeking to take the 'wisdom of God' and turn it into
'useful and applicable' information. You will be tempted, like so many stu-
dents before you, to simply absorb the information Jesus places before
you, to learn by acquiring data, tidbits stored neatly and precisely, with
all the other nuggets harvested and stored in the vastness of trivia that
bogs down the mind.

You will discover, perhaps already have, that Jesus has no interest
in trivia, that endless, useless pile of data that collects dust in the mind.
He will simply wait, ever so patiently, for you to act on the data you do
have, generating the questions of application that demonstrate an intent
to be 'transformed' by the data that Jesus is providing. The Serving King
has no patience for trivia in the mind of those trekking after Him. The
'truth' will indeed set you free (John 8:32), but only as it takes flight in
the everyday realities of those trekking after the Serving King.

Asking the questions of 'application' is the hard part, stymying us, rendering us moot before God in our silence, for knowledge without application is simply worthless. God will not provide truth for tomorrow until truth
for today has been put into play. So God goes silent, waiting patiently
for today's questions concerning how to implement 'this' or 'that' truth
from today. And no, dear friends, you will probably not receive wisdom
for those other trekkers journeying along with you, "the only thing God
intends to be clear is the way God deals with your own soul." Trek on.
There is so much more yet to discover concerning your soul.

21

Day 14

DID YOU HEAR THAT?

**"Whom shall I send? And who will go for Us?" And I said,
"Here am I. Send me!"
(Isaiah 6:8)**

"Get out of your mind the idea of expecting God to come with compulsions and pleadings." – Oswald Chambers

The simplicity and clarity of God's spoken word will surprise you; a voice quietly, yet profoundly, speaking into your mind, your heart, your inner most being. A voice that slips into your vocabulary, your voice, your life experience, your 'Sitz im Leben', and simply asks, "Who will go for Us" and do? In that moment, God will rarely use your name, for the 'question' is generic and open ended, and it is spoken to the 'many', not simply the 'one'. It is an open invitation to any and all who would trek after the King. You must come to understand it is an invitation to be 'first in line' for the opportunity and anointing that God provides.

That, of course, is the problem. The lack of specificity will provide you an escape, freeing you from having to respond to a generic question, a question that probes into the heart and mind of so many. You will be tempted to say, "Surely, someone else will do that. If God wanted me specifically, God would have called me by name; but God didn't, so I will let someone else do 'that.'" The 'other', that rare 'one' who decides to be 'first in line', will receive the blessing that God intended for so many, more importantly, intended for you.

Isaiah was 'first in line', "Here I am, send me!" What a privilege to 'hear' the voice of God, speaking words of invitation, words within 'ear-shot' of your mind. As you have discovered, God does not come with 'compulsions and pleadings', nor does God linger amongst those who 'hear' but never respond. God will simply move through the crowd, calling, creating opportunity for those who dare to hear, and then respond, "Here I am, send me!" And yes, there are endless opportunities to be 'first in line', for God creates a 'line' for each one of us. You need only step up and join Isaiah, "Here am I, send me!" Did you hear that?

Day 15
DEAD AND BURIED

We were therefore buried with Him through baptism into death in order that, just as Christ was raised from the dead through the glory of the Father, we too may live a new life.
(Romans 6:4)

"No one enters into the experience of entire sanctification without going through a 'white funeral'—the burial of the old life.'"—Oswald Chambers

'Sanctification', that which God does, as compared to 'consecration', that which we do, comes later in the journey for most. The latter is the simple reality of the 'death rattle', those last gasps of air from the dying 'old you', clinging to fading life in those final moments. The 'old you' does not pass quietly into the night. No such luxury for the child of God trekking after the Serving King. Instead, the 'old you' flees deep into the recesses of your inner being, hiding in the flesh, searching out concealed dark corners of body and soul, quietly abiding in the shadows, praying God will not find it, now that you have invited God to 'bury' any remains of the 'old you' that can be found.

Eventually, God finds those final pieces of the 'old you' hiding deep within, and pauses to validate, yet again, your desire to see the 'old you' die, piece by piece, if necessary, buried once and for all, freeing the 'new you' to blossom and be all that God has called you to be. Like all the newborns, the 'infant new you' will be inexperienced at this 'new life'. The 'new you' will stumble, as do all newborns, and you will be tempted to say, "The old me is still alive, still rumbling around in there, still dragging me into 'ways of being' I thought I had left behind, buried." Never confuse stumbling in your 'new life' on wobbly legs with sabotage by the 'old you'.

The 'old you' has been buried piece by piece, as the Spirit of God moves throughout your being, seeking out every last vestige of the 'old you'. Expect those 'wobbly' new legs to stumble along for a time as they seek new ways of 'being and doing'. The seemingly permanent stains of the old ways of 'being and doing' will fade with time, lifted by the presence of God. Practice will make the 'new life' seem as natural as did the 'old life'. It will take much practice, perhaps even a lifetime. Walk on in the 'newness of life'. Your trek into new ways of 'being and doing' is just beginning.

Day 16
ONLY YOU

**Then I heard the voice of the Lord saying,
"Whom shall I send?"
(Isaiah 6:8)**

"There are strands of the call of God providentially at work for us which we recognize and no one else does. It is the threading of God's voice to us in some particular matter, and it is no use consulting anyone else about it. We have to keep that profound relationship between our souls and God."–
Oswald Chambers

It is God's voice in the 'particular matter' that startles the unexpecting child of God, long accustomed to the safety of 'generic' calls to the 'many'. The voice startles because it is so specific, so clear, so particular, so unmistakably meant for you, and only you. You will wonder how He found you in the midst of the many? Moderns are used to generic teaching, words on a page everyone can comment on, evaluate, compare with others, and eventually 'wiggle' around by way of this or that. No such 'wiggle room' in that moment of 'particularity' from God. It is that stunning moment in the very presence of God as God's voice, that unmistakable voice, speaks directly into your being, naming you in ways only God can.

You will be tempted in that moment of 'particularity' to seek confirmation from those around you, "Did you hear what I heard?" You will run to the pages of God's preciously spoken Word to look for further affirmation, but confirmation will not come beyond that moment of 'particularity' with God, for such clarity need no further confirmation. Others will not hear it. Only you will hear it and confirmation is not needed, simply because you 'know' you have heard from the living God.

Then silence, a deafening silence, a silence that waits for you to respond, a response that no one will hear other than the One who has spoken into your 'particular'. Isaiah simply responds, "Hear I am Lord, send me." It is a glorious moment for those fortunate enough, blessed enough, to have God speak to their 'particular'. It will not be the last time God speaks to your particular. Your journey, your sending, your hearing the voice of "Him who calls" has just begun. There are many more moments of clarity yet ahead for those who dare to move forward in obedience. Trek on...

Day 17
THE LONELY PATH

But when God, who set me apart from birth and called me by His grace, was pleased to reveal His Son in me so that I might preach Him among the Gentiles, I did not consult any man...
(Galatians 1:15-16)

"The call of God is not a call to any particular service; my interpretation of it may be..."– Oswald Chambers

The 'arrogance of certainty', that moment in which the voice and direction of God is so unmistakably clear, will tempt you to "not consult any man." Clearly, there are those moments, a 'Pauline moment', rare as it may be, in which 'consultation' is not needed, nor ought to be utilized. Clarity from God ought not be subjected to the voices of doubt. Recognize that you are not the first, nor the last, to be 'called' into service out of your devotion to God. Many have gone before you in response to the 'call' of 'Him Who calls'. They, those who have gathered, that band of followers, who do 'consult' one another, offer lifetimes of experience about 'trekking after Jesus', the Serving King. And those stories ought to be heard.

However, those who 'trek after Jesus' can do no more than tell you about 'their' unique journey with Him. They cannot provide you a precise roadmap for your journey, for no two journeys, like no two fingerprints, are ever the same, thus Paul's confession, "I did not consult any man." Consultation would do you no good. Another cannot tell you about 'your journey', for it is uniquely yours as you trek along the Serving King's path, designed uniquely for you.

The stories of the 'other' journeys will prove invaluable. Their stories will give you insight into yours. But be warned, you cannot make their stories yours. Theirs is not a path to be 'trekked along on'; to the contrary, each path is fresh and new, designed for the 'one', and only 'one', who must walk along it. Thus, sooner or later, you must leave the comfort of the 'band of brothers' and walk alone, 'consulting' no one, walking in solitude along the path that waits ahead. This is indeed the finest moment of faith. It is the road to "job well done good and faithful servant." Trek on...

Day 18

OBEDIENCE IN THE DARK

Thomas said to Him, "My Lord and my God!"
(John 20:28)

"...and unbribed devotion to the Lord Jesus, a satisfaction to Him wherever He places us."– Oswald Chambers

Some things about Jesus, things like, 'He is alive and moving amongst us', are just too difficult to comprehend, in spite of the pleas from those we have long journeyed with. It is easy to analyze the stories about Jesus, to apply the principles of Jesus, but affirming His presence, His 'right hereness', right-now presence, is a far different matter, especially if all one has to go on is the testimony of others, even trusted others. Even Thomas found it difficult to affirm the testimony of trusted friends.

You will have to embrace that reality from time to time, those uncomfortable moments, when everyone else seems to have 'seen' Him, everyone but you. It is in those moments that you must decide, "Whom will I trust? Who is worthy of my trust? Can I walk in the confidence of someone else's encounter with the resurrected Christ?" Thomas had learned to trust no one's encounter but his own, "I will never believe!" (John 20:25). Sadly, many will follow his example and miss so much of what God has in store.

Jesus often speaks to the 'others' in your life, and you will have to endure the unpleasant reality that you have been placed in the 'dark', in a room where everyone seems to have seen and heard from Jesus, everyone but you. In those moments you will be tempted to allow fear and envy to rob you of obedience and the blessing that Jesus intends for you in the 'obedience of the dark'. But there are options. You can simply embrace the words of Jesus, "Blessed are those who have not seen and yet have believed" (John 20:29). In that moment, you will not only experience the joy of obedience to Jesus, but the gift of 'confidence in another', sharing a rich relationship with the One Whom you have trusted. Who are the 'others' that you have learned to trust as you trek on?

Day 19
AND SO WE SLEEP

**As the sun was going down, a deep sleep fell on Abram. And behold, dreadful and great darkness fell upon him.
(Genesis 15:12)**

"When God gives a vision and darkness follows, wait. God will make you in accordance with the vision He has given if you will wait His time. Never try and help God fulfill His word..."– Oswald Chambers

Never confuse what God announces God will do with what God announces you should do. The two are clearly different experiences and to confuse them, to mistake the latter for the former, will create chaos for both you and those who trek alongside you in your trek after the Serving King. That, of course, leads to those horrible moments of darkness, the inability to see how God is going to do what only God can do, what God has revealed God will do. The deafening silence and blinding darkness will combine to render you 'helpless' in the fullest sense of the word.

Panic will slowly creep into your spirit if you are not careful, even intentional, in your continued stillness before God. Your flesh will scream, "Do something! Anything!" Worse, the 'something', the 'anything', will flash so clearly in your mind, it will urge you to action, to assist, to help God; but you must resist, sit still, tolerating the silence and darkness. However, 'chaos' is rarely silent in the darkness that surrounds you. You will hear it, clamoring all around you, begging you to come and silence it, to 'act' in the absence of God, to bring a calming presence to the 'chaos'. 'Chaos' will remind you that only you can usher in the peace that is needed so badly, relentlessly clamoring, "You are the 'one.'"

Your spirit must resist. You are not the 'one'. In that moment of darkness and silence, you must wait, ever so patiently, for God to act. In that moment you must "Be still and know that I am God" (Psalm 46:10). Sleep in the 'great darkness', for it is in the 'great darkness' that God is at God's best. Hide in the comfort of that 'deep sleep' while God goes about being God. Trek on in the stillness of the darkness all around you.

Day 20

YOU CAN'T FORGET THIS ONE

**"...unless one is born again he cannot see the kingdom of God."
(John 3:3)**

"Being born again from above is a perennial, perpetual and eternal beginning, a freshness all the time in thinking and in talking and in living, the continual surprise of the life of God."– Oswald Chambers

Our lack of memory concerning 'birth' is problematic, robbing us of the uncomfortable, perhaps even unpleasant or painful recollections of the process of moving from the warmth and safety of the womb into the harsh realities awaiting us outside the womb. We hear the words of Jesus with no ability to understand the trauma awaiting those who 'brave' the call to be 'born again'. Nor do we remember the pain and trauma for 'mother', her willingness to 'bear' with us, to carry us, to pay any price, to 'usher' us into life.

The 'birth from above' will offer us no such memory lapse, no blissful entrance into 'new life'. No, it is a far different journey for those who 'brave' this being 'born again'. You will 'know' the cost to others of your being 'born again'. The cross will stand ever before you, a constant reminder of the pain of Him who 'birthed you', bothering you more than you could ever anticipate. You will be tempted to look away, to embrace the joy of forgetfulness, leaving the cost of your 'birth' to romanticized pictures of 'mother on the cross'; but this time, you know, really know, the 'perennial and eternal beginning' of the price that was paid for your being 'born again'. There will be no forgetting the pangs of childbirth this time around.

Resist the temptation to look away. The pangs of childbirth ought never fade from sight, not even for a moment. See your 'mother' as He 'bears' the burden of your being 'born again'. Embrace the memory. Own it. Your birth was more costly than you could have ever dreamed. Still, the Serving King paid the price, deemed you worthy of the sacrifice, every moment of agony. It is His gift to you.

However, the memory comes with an obligation, the call to honor Him who birthed you. So the purpose of the trek after the Serving King appears. Trek on in honor of Him Who birthed you.

Day 21
DEVOTION OF A DIFFERENT KIND

"I remember the devotion of your youth..."
(Jeremiah 2:2)

"Am I as full of the extravagance of love to Jesus Christ as I was in the beginning, when I went out of my way to prove my devotion to Him?"– Oswald Chambers

Youthful devotion is full of 'emotion' and 'spontaneity' and it seems to flow effortlessly and easily toward the 'object' of that devotion. As those who have survived it know, youthful devotion is fleeting at best, if it 'remains' in the realm of 'emotional' exuberance. Sustaining 'devotion' is tricky, it requires an ability to 'love' beyond the 'knowledge' of intimacy. It is this 'knowledge' from intimacy that threatens 'youthful devotion' and its idealized images of the 'object of devotion'. Intimacy comes with that 'long walk of life' eventually revealing the true character and 'details of reality' concerning the 'object of devotion'. It is then that you will discover the waning of your 'youthful devotion'.

Discovering the 'real God' will rattle your 'youthful devotion' as the 'idealized' God is replaced with images of 'Who', not 'What', God really is. Like all persons who have been the 'object' of your youthful devotion, God will not neatly fit into your objectified personification of Him; instead, reality of personhood will continually alter your personified images. And that, of course, will nibble away at your youthful devotion, as 'reality' replaces 'personified images' with a reality that is not nearly so accommodating as your carefully crafted reflections of 'Who' and 'What' you desire God to be. You do not get to 'craft' your own God.

Then will come that moment, a moment that repeats with each new insight into the reality of 'Who' God is, a moment requiring you to 'embrace fully' the completeness of the reality of God, a moment requiring surrender of 'hopes and wishes' replaced by the 'realities' of the true living God. A new devotion arises from the ashes of your 'youthful devotion', a far different thing than that which preceded it. Yes, it will be 'different', vastly different, than its predecessor, but it will be rooted in the reality of the Living God, not the wishful thinking of youthful dreams and wants. It is this 'older devotion' that will sustain you long after 'youthful devotions' have died. Trek on...

Day 22
WHAT DO YOU SEE?

"Turn to Me and be saved..."
(Isaiah 45:22)

"Troubles nearly always make us look to God; His blessings are apt to make us look elsewhere."– Oswald Chambers

The arrogance of self-sufficiency thrives in those moments of prosperity, moments creating an illusion suggesting "I have done this thing," an illusion that will carry on long after the 'conditions' that gave birth to such illusions have disappeared. Eventually, conditions do change, forcing each of us to come to that horrible moment in which 'turning to God' is the only option left; no person escapes the finality of this life.

Isaiah, still stuck in the illusion, has not yet learned to "look unto Me," he is still 'looking' into the conditions, the circumstances of life, rising and falling with each changing tide. Breaking out of the 'illusion' requires a concerted effort. It begins with the surrendering of 'lip service' in a nod toward God, using the language of 'God credit' all the while secretly harboring the illusion of 'self achievement'. Worse yet is the 'illusion' of reward, that somehow the conditions of your life are a reward for your 'faithfulness toward God'. Illusions of this sort are especially hard to break free from.

Once liberated from the 'illusion', the shame of having lived in the 'illusion' for so very long will threaten to keep you from looking up into the face of Him Who has blessed you, chosen you, readied you for this very moment. You must push through your shame and find God's face, the face of God's Son, the One who can and does truly 'save you'. When you find that face, fear not the noise of the chaos around you. It serves only to remind you that chaos can never 'save you', never redeem you, never give you the life you so desperately desire. That life, that freedom from the concerns of the chaos around you, is found only in Him. As the hymn writer suggested so long ago, "Turn your eyes upon Jesus, look full in His wonderful face, and the things of earth will go strangely dim..." (Helen H. Lemmel, 1922).

Day 23
POLISHING THE MIRROR

And we all, with unveiled face, beholding the glory of the Lord, are being transformed into the same image.
(2 Corinthians 3:18)

"The outstanding characteristic of a Christian is this unveiled frankness before God so that the life becomes a mirror for other lives..."– Oswald Chambers

'Frankness' before God is never easy, especially if this 'frankness' entails more than a superficial 'God peek' into the real you. What if God's intention is to redeem and reclaim you in such a profound fashion that you begin to reflect God's very being as would a mirror, as did Moses (Exodus 34:35): the mirror affect.

It is the mirroring of 'Godness' that seems too optimistic for most of us. We have become so accustomed to the 'dullness' of our 'fallenness', the hope for radical transformation quietly died, killing much, if not all, of our hope of 'reflecting the glory of God'. The 'veil' has become such a part of our daily wardrobe that daring to take it off before God seems too risky. However, it is the risk you must take if you are to ever reflect the glory of God.

This risk of unveiling is more comprehensive than you have imagined. This willingness to 'unveil', for both God and neighbor, allowing those around you to see what you have tried to hide for so very many years, from both God and 'neighbor'. Unveiling for 'neighbor' allows 'neighbor' to see not just the 'reflection of the Living God', but just as importantly, the 'mirror' itself, tarnished, even cracked in places. Those willing to 'unveil' have come to realize the mirror has not been perfected, nor shall it be; rather, polished, so finely polished, so the very being of God can be seen reflecting off the surfaces of the real you, the you that has been hiding. The 'veil' hindering the polishing for so very long that you had forgotten its power to reflect, to shine when touched by the grace of God. The unveiling is a difficult step for the child of God, but fear not. Take off the veil and let God's image reflect off the 'you' that has been. Trek on...

Day 24
WAS IT PASSING?

**"But rise and stand upon your feet, for I have appeared
to you for this purpose..."
(Acts 26:16)**

*"The vision Paul had on the road to Damascus was no passing
emotion..."– Oswald Chambers*

Paul's encounter with the 'Risen Lord' did not occur in the peaceful bliss and comfort of a local church, angelic choirs singing Amazing Grace as the organ serenades; to the contrary, he was literally rocked from his animal and blinded into submission. Jesus simply informed Paul of "what you must do" (Acts 9:6 NIV). Thus, little wonder Paul adopted the term 'slave' to describe the foundation of his 'loving' relationship with the 'Risen Lord'. Servant is the title used for those who freely choose to serve. Slave is reserved for a privileged few overpowered in the most miraculous manner by the loving force of the Serving King.

'Emotion' will not sustain the servant, or even the slave, who treks into hardship following the path Jesus has appointed, or stands before the accusers, those who question both the 'call' and the 'resolve' to stay faithful to His beckoning. 'Emotion' birthed in the comfort of the 'like-minded' simply cannot sustain the child of God in the company of the 'unlike-minded'. Only an encounter with the 'Risen Lord' can provide the tenacity of relationship needed for the company of the 'unlike-minded'. Therein lies the problem.

The 'encounter', regardless of how 'dramatic and profound' it may have been, will not sustain you for years on end. No, the encounter requires the daily reinforcement of the One Who first called and demanded. It is that frequent encounter that sustains one's call and commitment to the journey. Unlike that first capturing, future encounters will depend on the captured 'slave of God' freely returning to the feet of the Master. Only those repeated visits into the presence of Him Who calls will sustain you long after the 'emotion' has died. The Serving King waits. The trek is just beginning.

Day 25
WHEN IT PLEASES

But when He who had set me apart before I was born, and Who called me by His grace, was pleased to reveal His Son to me... (Galatians 1:15)

"Always be in a state of expectancy, and see that you leave room for God to come in as He likes."– Oswald Chambers

Paul was very deep into his trek after the Serving King when it 'pleased' God to show Paul the deeper and more profound aspects of trekking after God. You will have to get used to this 'pleased God', if you are to last in your quest for intimacy with God. Searching for knowledge, applying knowledge, and even demanding more knowledge, are all important aspects of growing in one's knowledge of God, but they will not, in and of themselves, usher in 'intimate knowledge' of God. Some things, perhaps many things, can only be 'received' when God is 'pleased to reveal'.

Yes, it is that 'waiting until it pleased God' that will cause you pause in your trekking after God. You will be tempted to assign blame for your lack of insight. However, there is no blame to be found; rather, sometimes, it simply has not 'pleased God' to make known to you the more intimate details of the treasury of God's knowledge. 'Pleased God' is far more complicated than you could ever imagine. Understanding God's timing can be an exasperating process for those trekking after the Serving King. God's ways are simply not our ways, nor God's timing our timing.

Then, when it is least expected, God is 'pleased to reveal' in a manner that will demand you lay down much, if not all, of what you have previously 'known' of God. Such moments of revelation create chaos as you attempt to assimilate the 'new' with the 'old', now that it 'pleased God'. Paul, blinded by this new revelation of God, can only wait until it 'pleased God' to remove the 'scales', allowing Paul to see more than he could have ever imagined. Are you prepared to 'see' that which will invalidate much of your previous 'sightings' of God? Or have you placed God neatly in your well-organized world? Trek on, there is much ahead that God will be 'pleased to reveal'.

Day 26
CARING FOR FEATHERS

**"But if God so clothes the grass of the field, which today is alive and tomorrow is thrown into the oven, will He not much more clothe you, O you of little faith?"
(Matthew 6:30)**

"Jesus says that if you are rightly related to Him and obey this Spirit that is in you, God will look after your feathers."– Oswald Chambers

'Caring for feathers' is a full-time job slowly presenting itself as maturity creeps its way into our lives, the bliss of childhood fading into the distance. By the time we become adults, 'feather caring' has become as natural to us as breathing. His announcement, "My Father will care for your feathers," presents the arrival of a delightful arrangement, or so you think. However, you will soon discover God's 'feather care' is a far different thing than your 'feather care'.

So the trek after the Serving King takes on a brand new twist, a willingness to trek anywhere with Him precisely because of your confidence in 'feathers' being cared for. But understand, God's 'feather caring' rarely looks like yours. His ways are not your ways, especially when it comes to caring for 'feathers'. The 'many', not understanding His way of 'feather care', will assume they are not 'rightly related' to God, otherwise 'feather care' would proceed according to plan. That is usually not the case; instead, the simple reality that God's 'feather care' is radically different from our 'feather care'.

So you discover you long ago abandoned 'feather care' in God's way, focused care given to the 'feathers' that matter, the 'feathers' that enable flight; instead, grooming the 'feathers' of 'pomp and circumstance', the plume, pretty but useless in the long-running battle of life. God ignores those 'feathers' of 'pomp and circumstance' grand as they may be for parading around the town square, but useless in the battles yet to come. They must be plucked and tossed to the ground, no longer of value to those trekking after the Serving King. Fear not, "God will look after your feathers." It is God's way. Feathers that have been cared for by God are more than ready for battle, for the flight yet ahead of you. Move forward with reckless abandon. God is faithful. Your 'feathers' will be well cared for. Trek on...

Day 27
SOIL OF THE SOUL

"Therefore I tell you, do not be anxious about your life..."
(Matthew 6:25)

"A warning which needs to be reiterated is that the cares of this world, the deceitfulness of riches, and the lust of other things entering in, will choke all that God puts in. We are never free from the recurring tides of this encroachment."–
Oswald Chambers

The relentless 'encroachment' of the cares of this life find power, not in an overwhelming assault upon our deepest needs, but rather a perpetual chipping, a chipping that is rarely felt, painlessly eroding the 'soil' in which the character of God is desperately trying to take root deep within your being. They do not assault the character of God directly, clearly a waste of time, for the character of God established in you cannot be eroded. No, the relentless assault is upon the 'soil of the soul' in which the character of God is attempting to sink deep into life-changing roots.

Nor are the relentless waves 'bad' or 'evil', in and of themselves. To the contrary, these ever-pounding waves of desire are the very 'desires' and 'wants' God planted deep within you, but they are 'rogue waves' amplified by a steady and relentless pounding from the culture around you which feeds and thrives on your dependence upon 'things', rather than God as the source of contentment and peace.

Tragically, the 'tides of encroachment' do not lessen with each passing day, rather they crash upon the 'soil of the soul' in each and every moment of life. The child of God will have to learn those vital 'erosion protection techniques' that replenish the 'soil of soul' on a daily basis. Erosion will occur. Protection will never be enough, replacement must happen. The child of God will have to find those 'erosion buffets' and this will not be easy, for the terrain of the soil is different for each one trekking after the Serving King. You will be tempted to mimic the 'erosion prevention techniques' that others have found powerful and effective. In the end, no two soils are ever the same; hence, nor can be the techniques that replenish and protect that precious 'soil of the soul'. Are you protecting the 'soil of the soul' as you trek on?

Day 28
YESTERDAY'S MESSAGE

**"Saul, Saul, why are you persecuting Me?
It is hard for you to kick against the goads."
(Acts 26:14)**

"...and when the knowledge comes home that it is Jesus Whom we have been persecuting all the time, it is the most crushing revelation there could be." – Oswald Chambers

Living in accord with 'yesterday's message' is rarely the right way of functioning. It is startling, horribly shocking, even traumatizing, to discover you have been in 'yesterday's message' for so long that, rather than serving God, you have been 'persecuting' God, hurting God. You will say, "How can that be, I am simply doing what God told me to do yesterday?" Therein lies the point. It was God's message for 'yesterday', not today. You will protest even further, "But that cannot be, God is the same today, yesterday and tomorrow." Thus is the tragedy of confusing the 'being of God' with the 'message of God'.

Saul knows the scandal and agony of discovering a life lived in 'yesterday's message'. He has been 'blinded' by 'yesterday's message', yesterday's calling, rendering him useless; no, much worse than useless, rather painful to God, attempting to stymie the very work of God, stumbling along with eyes blinded by 'yesterday's message'. Saul discovers he is now contrary to the will of God. However, God's grace is always ready to cure our blindness when 'it pleases God' to do so.

So God ushers in a new 'blindness' for Saul, a blindness that will ultimately, should he surrender to it, give him 'eyes to see' a new message, 'today's message'. Saul will never be the same, seeing with such clarity and transformation that a name change is at hand. Paul is birthed again, by the power of his new vision, and his steadfastness from that day forward to live in 'today's message', never 'yesterday's message'. Sadly, too many will fear the trauma of hearing 'today's message', requiring a profound change of course, or more importantly, a change of 'being'. When was the last time you heard 'today's message'? The child of God seeking to trek after the Serving King must be ready for radical 'change of course' at any given moment. Trek on...

Day 29
WHO ARE YOU?

And I said, "Who are You, Lord?"
(Acts 26:15)

"God has to destroy our determined confidence in our own convictions. 'I know this is what I should do'—and suddenly the voice of God speaks in a way that overwhelms us by revealing the depths of our ignorance. We have shown our ignorance of Him in the very way we determined to serve Him."—Oswald Chambers

Saul, early in his youth, devoted himself to the ways of God, and, like so many of us, soon found the 'ways of his youth' impossible to leave behind. Thus, God could no longer speak to him in any 'form' outside of his 'youthful ways'. No wonder then that Paul, upon encountering the Risen Lord, had to ask, "Who are You, Lord?" Yesterday's message often clouds today's.

The child of God determined to trek after the Serving King will learn God rarely intends to speak with us in the 'forms' of our youth. Further, 'youthfulness' is any day other than today. You will be tempted to say, "God liked 'this' yesterday, so God must like 'this' today." Don't allow your absolute conviction of what God intended for you and with you yesterday to be God's intent for your tomorrow. That, of course, makes trekking after the Serving King a moment-by-moment adventure, ever unpredictable and changing for the child who stays in intimate conversation with God.

Nonetheless, it is the 'determined convictions' from yesterday that prevent us from recognizing the 'Lord' in the freshness of a new moment. Further, those 'determined convictions' from yesterday prevent us from hearing His voice in the commands and circumstances of the new moment. You will have to be wary of allowing 'yesterday's determined convictions' from becoming 'today's hardened old ways of being and doing'. Hold loosely to the 'convictions of yesterday' for God may have a fresh and new direction for you today. Saul changes course only when he realizes Who this 'Lord' of the present moment really is. Listen carefully for His voice. He may shock you with 'course corrections' causing you to pause and ask, "Is that You, Lord?" And when you discover it is He in this new moment, trek on into today's moment.

<h1 style="text-align:center">Day 30</h1>

WHO CAN BEAR SUCH NEWS

**And Samuel was afraid to tell the vision to Eli.
(1 Samuel 3:15)**

"Never ask the advice of another about anything God makes you decide before Him. If you ask advice, you will nearly always side with Satan..."– Oswald Chambers

For the child of God in tune with the heart and mind of God, hearing God will not be an unusual event. When others discover you 'hear from God', do not be surprised when they call upon you, just as Eli beckoned unto Samuel to fetch a message from God. Samuel does indeed hear from God regarding Eli, but the message is anything but pleasant, "Therefore I swear to the house of Eli that the iniquity of Eli's house shall not be atoned for by sacrifice or offering forever." Like Samuel, you will be tempted to be silent, silent for a very long time, as long a time as possible, rather than be the bearer of tragic news.

Worse yet, comes the temptation to rest in the promises to others, the grace that is intended for another, the promise of better tomorrows, surrendered long ago through disobedience by the one who seeks to hear from God through you. For who among us seeks to be the bearer of bad news for those who have lived as foolishly as Eli? But to those who ask, fear not being the bearer of God's announcement, even the rejection of any future "sacrifice or offering."

Never confuse the advice sought by another with a call to be the voice of God to 'any and all' whom dwell in your proximity. The latter is a special calling, known only to the few, the prophets whom God has set aside to speak without caution or concern, throwing God's decrees to the open air. For the rest of us, focus on God's prophetic message for your journey, that moment-by-moment attempt to live all of life centered in the will of God. When God speaks in that 'custom-made' revelation that is precisely and only for you, do not hesitate to receive what God has given you. "Never ask the advice of another about anything God makes you decide before Him." Yours is simply to receive and do as you trek on.

Day 31

A DIVINE SEPARATION

...set apart for the gospel of God.
(Romans 1:1)

"Paul did not say he separated himself, but–'when it pleased God who separated me.'"– Oswald Chambers

Some will simply choose to 'trek after God', and will do so, moment by moment throughout a lifetime. Others, like Paul, do not 'choose' at all; rather, they are claimed, set apart, stripped of 'choosing' altogether, told what 'you must do' (Acts 9:6). Never confuse being 'set apart' by God with 'choosing to be set apart'. The latter, wonderful and praise-worthy as it may be, is constantly threatened by the 'worries of life' and 'distractions' of all kinds.

The former, however, is a perpetual state of being, an everlasting condition, created and established by the 'will of Him Who was pleased to separate', to claim you as His very own. Still, for the one who has 'chosen' God, 'willfully' following in each new moment by moment, there is another way, a capturing by the Serving King. It is the way of 'separation' that 'pleased God' in creating a glorious moment of sanctification for Saul.

However, being 'set aside' for God's use only, often, perhaps even always, comes only after the 'willful follower' has utterly surrendered 'all' unto the cause of Christ. It is that 'willful consecration', not to be confused with sanctification (that which only God can do), preparing the way for God's gracious response of separation, a separation that renders one, fully and completely, God's very own. Even an amazing second work of grace is not 'comprehensive', for it does not redeem the 'body of flesh' which continues to die around the 'inner being'. No, the liberation of which Paul speaks is a redemptive healing of the 'inner being' (Romans 7:22), even as the flesh (soma) continues its unpleasant decay and conse-quent war against the 'sanctified life'. How will you know when the inner being has been 'separated' by God and for God? "For I delight in the Law of God in my inner being..." (Romans 7:22). Have you the 'delight' that only comes when it has 'pleased God' to set you apart? Trek on...

Day 32
PLEADING AGAIN?

Christ did not send me to baptize but to preach the gospel...
(1 Corinthians 1:17)

"If God were human, how sick to the heart and weary He would be of the constant requests we make for our salvation, for our sanctification. We tax His energies from morning till night for things for ourselves–something for me to be delivered from! When we touch the bedrock of the reality of the Gospel of God, we shall never bother God any further with little personal plaints."–Oswald Chambers

For the child of God trekking after the Serving King fast as humanly possible, it is hard to resist pleading with God, "Slowdown" or "Quicken my step!" The child of God is often consumed with "what a wretched man I am" (Romans 7:24), precisely because your 'trekking after the Serving King' has brought you closer and closer into God's very presence, within sight of God's very being, enabling you to 'know' Who God really is, and how utterly 'not' you are in comparison. The discontinuity between you and God, even in the midst of your 'very best' moments of 'being and doing', are simply unbearable to the 'saint' radically determined to find 'transformation into the image of God's Son'.

Then the 'scales of your Damascus Road' experience fall by the wayside as you suddenly realize this is not about me, and my being 'lifted up', but, rather, Him being 'lifted up" (John 12:32), even in the midst of my 'weakness'. For the child of God radically committed to 'transformation', glorying in weakness is never easy; rather, horrifying and humiliating, and more so the longer into the trek one has been.

It is in those moments, when you are most tempted to plead with Father one more time to make you 'all that you can be', that you must pause and hear the words of Jesus once again, "But if God so clothes the grass of the field, which today is alive and tomorrow is thrown into the oven, will He not much more clothe you, O you of little faith" (John 6:30)? You need not continue to bother your loving Father. God knows how best to 'clothe' those determined to trek after Him. Simply walk on behind Him Who has called you. God will clothe you at precisely the right moment, or God will not. Yours is simply to trust in God who 'clothes' when and how 'God is pleased to do so'. Trek on...

40

Day 33
WOE OF A SPECIAL KIND

Woe to me if I do not preach the gospel!
(I Corinthians 9:16)

To be "separated unto the gospel" means to hear the call of God; and when a man begins to overhear that call, then begins agony that is worthy of the name. Every ambition is nipped in the bud, every desire of life quenched, every outlook completely extinguished and blotted out, saving one thing only– "separated unto the gospel." Woe be to the soul who tries to put his foot in any other direction when once that call has come to him.– Oswald Chambers

Few ever hear this 'call of God', a stunning realization you ought to do 'no other thing' than to surrender every other ambition in life to serving the One Who has 'called'. Be not surprised when the 'others', who have 'heard that call', are leery of your certainty. They know the irreversible 'calling of Him Who is pleased' and the utter joy awaiting those breaking free from all that which 'so easily entangles' (Hebrews 12:1) the 'beautiful feet' (Romans 10:15) of those whose 'ambitions' have not been 'nipped in the bud' and 'completely extinguished'.

It is the 'easy entanglements' of life's ambitions creating the 'woe' of which Paul alludes. The 'woes' are, in and of themselves, not the fundamental source of misery for the 'called-out ones'; no, it is the lack of joy dogging you in the midst of all those 'ambitions and joys' that used to fill your life with meaning and delight. Those 'called' suddenly discover 'life' apart from 'living and being' the Gospel is now grey and colorless, lackluster and dull, pointless to the point of being a painful 'woe'.

Thus, those 'called' can no longer 'live' as they have before, dancing with Gospel when the music is right, dancing with 'others' when it is not. Avoiding 'woe' is not hard for the child of God called 'when it pleased' God; but 'living and being' Gospel will take time to get used it. Learn early in this journey that 'woe' is patient, very patient, content to follow behind you for decades, waiting for that opportune moment when you are most tempted to leave 'Gospel' behind, for just a moment, ever so brief a moment, in the journey of life. Your dance with 'woe' will begin yet again, for 'woe' never tires of waiting. But be of good cheer. 'Gospel' graciously waits patiently as well. 'Joy' always follows wherever 'Gospel' is taken.

Day 34
MIRE OF A SPECIAL KIND

**We have become, and are still, like the scum of the world, the refuse of all things.
(I Corinthians 4:13)**

"We have discreet affinities that keep us out of the mire— 'I won't stoop; I won't bend.' You do not need to, you can be saved by the skin of your teeth if you like..."— Oswald Chambers

For the child of God trekking after the Serving King, heading into the 'mire' was not the intended destination, at least for most; rather, the hopefulness of getting 'out of the mire', a 'mire' that has long bogged the children of God down, robbing them of the vitality and life God intends for His children. However, the 'mire' into which God leads is a 'mire' of a far different kind than the 'mire' left behind. The 'mire' of God, so called by those who have not 'heard' the calling of 'God Who was pleased', is not 'mire' to the 'called one'; but rather to those watching the 'life experiences' of the 'called one'. The 'watchers' Paul points to are not those outside the Body of Christ, rather, those 'inside' the Body of Christ.

Thus, Paul proclaims, "that God has exhibited us Apostles as last of all" (I Corinthians 4:9). There the 'called ones' find their 'stumbling block', their "I won't stoop, I won't bend"; it is in serving those who 'value not' the 'stooping and bending' of the 'called ones'. Suddenly, the 'called-out one' realizes with great horror, a 'mire' of a different kind, a 'mire' sucking the joy and vitality of 'being and doing Gospel', a 'mire' that threatens the very 'irrevocable calling' of 'God who was pleased'.

The 'called one' will sink without constant 'eyes upon Jesus', as one walks in the 'calling'. But with 'eyes upon Jesus', the 'called one' will never see the 'mire', never notice the life-threatening muck, never know the sense of "last of all, never know life is being poured out as an offering"; rather, the 'called one' will stride with joy across the 'mire' others see, embraced in the joy of life-giving 'Gospel'. Trek on through the mire that is no more.

Day 35

A LATER LOVE

For the love of Christ controls us...
(2 Corinthians 5:14)

"Paul says he is overruled, overmastered, held as in a vice, by the love of Christ. Very few of us know what it means to be held in a grip by the love of God...and the strange thing is that it is the last thing realized by the Christian worker. Paul says he is gripped by the love of Christ."– Oswald Chambers

Trivialization of the 'call of God' is a well intended, but sadly misguided, attempt to create equality of relationship and experience for all God's children. Nothing could be further from the truth. Contrary to the masses who demand 'calling' be nothing more than responding to God's generic bellowing into the wind, like commoners coming to the King's feast (Matthew 22:1-14), the 'calling' that "overruled, overmastered, held as in a vice" ought never be confused with the 'common call' going out unto all people.

No, the 'calling' that controls is a very different thing, and very few ever hear it, much less find themselves "overmastered" by it. Fewer still trek so closely with 'God Who was pleased' that a new constraint, a powerful overmaster seizes the soul, gaining complete mastery over the 'inner being', ushering in a new reality of being that "delights in the Law of God" (Romans 7:21), replacing the old constraint with a new and overwhelming constraint, the constraint of love.

Few ever know that kind of love, the love of a person, rendering the lover powerless under its control. When the 'love of Christ' arrives, and Oswald Chambers is right, it is "the last thing realized" by the child trekking after God, it masters the 'lover' utterly and completely, so completely everything else in life becomes secondary, perhaps even unimportant and mundane.

You will have to resist the temptation to trivialize this kind of 'love', this 'calling' of a special kind as the crowd demands you return to the mob, dancing with Gospel, loving Jesus only when it is convenient, only when others hear the music as well. Resisting the mob will never be easy, but there is a special kind of 'love' waiting for those who 'hear' the King, who 'love' the King, and find the love that only comes late.

43

Day 36
NOBILITY OF ANOTHER KIND

Even if I am to be poured out as a drink offering upon the sacrificial offering of your faith, I am glad and rejoice with you all. (Philippians 2:17)

"Or do you say– 'I am not going to be offered up just yet, I do not want God to choose my work. I want to choose the scenery of my own sacrifice; I want to have the right kind of people watching me and saying, "Well done." Are you ready to be not so much as a drop in a bucket–to be so hopelessly insignificant that you are never thought of again in connection with the life you served?"– Oswald Chambers

The nobility of a 'life poured out' for the sake of another is only noble if the right people are watching, or so we think. For the child of God who has known the 'love that arrives late', a new kind of nobility arrives with such love. It is nobility much like the kind bestowed by the crowd of 'watchers', but the 'watchers' matter not, rather the 'Watcher' takes center stage. For the child of God who has been authentically captured by the 'love that arrives late', it will not matter that the crowd is no longer 'watching'; instead, only the great joy of knowing 'The Watcher' has, indeed, simply 'watched'.

That is the ironic twist of 'nobility' rooted in the calling of 'God Who was pleased'. Suddenly, it matters not if an audience can be found to watch a life "poured out as a drink offering"; instead, all that matters is that the 'Watcher,' the One Who called, is indeed watching and pleased by your offering. It is a 'nobility' that goes unnoticed, except by Him, the only One that matters.

You will be tempted to find the crowd from time to time, even if it is a 'crowd' of one other, just one other, seeing what the One, the Watcher sees. However, if you are to find the 'nobility of another kind', it must be done in solitude, the solitude that comes when your service is before an audience of the One, never two. Service in the solitude of the One will be harder than you can ever imagine. It may indeed require that moment of, "Even if I am to be poured out..." But if you are indeed fortunate enough to find that moment of 'solitude' with the One, embrace it, for it is the rarest of moments. Few find it, fewer still embrace it. Trek on...

Day 37
WATCHING THE FIRE

**For I am already being poured out as a drink offering...
(2 Timothy 4:6)**

"*You* do not destroy it, God does; you bind the sacrifice to the horns of the altar; and see that you do not give way to self-pity when the fire begins. After this way of fire, there is nothing that oppresses or depresses. – Oswald Chambers

No one really expects Isaac to die at the hands of Abraham. After all, the 'ram is in the thicket', thus the story so familiar it loses its power, its drama, its surprise ending, when suddenly, the ram struggles in the thicket, catching the eye of Abraham, and averting the death of Abraham's son; the tragedy of tales too familiar.

It will not take long in your trek after God before you learn that many of your sacrifices 'bound to the horns of the altar' will indeed go up in flames, for there is no 'ram' in the thicket. Your sacrifice is real and not intended to be a story for the world to see; no, often there will be no audience at all, other than the audience of the 'One' Who delights in the smell of yet another sacrifice burned in God's presence.

You will be tempted to think God must 'enjoy' the fragrance of yet another 'sacrifice' burned at the altar; but it is not the 'fragrance' of your sacrifice itself that brings a smile to God's face. No, it is the freedom from 'oppression or depression' that you have found that warms the heart of God. It is the freedom that comes your way as you watch the fire of your sacrifice and know you are still 'ok', even being 'poured out' cannot rob you of life; rather, it is birthing life deep within you. It is your new life bringing delight to the very being of God as He inhales the 'fragrance of sacrifice'.

Like the 'love that arrives late', this kind of sacrifice will come later in the trek after the Serving King. It is a freedom to 'be and do Gospel' without the constraints of 'stuff' hindering and fatiguing the spirit of the one trekking after the Serving King. But it will not burn spontaneously, you will have to 'bind the sacrifice to the horns of the altar'. Trek on...

Day 38

SPIRITUAL LUST

**But we trusted … and beside all this, today is the third day …
(Luke 24:21)**

*"Dejection springs from one of two sources – I have either sat-
isfied a lust or I have not. Lust means – I must have it at once.
Spiritual lust makes me demand an answer from God, instead
of seeking God Who gives the answer." – Oswald Chambers*

Overcoming 'lust', that sense of "I must have it at once," is rarely
thought of as a 'spiritual lust' or weakness; especially if the 'it' we lust
after is the very being of God. However, for the child of the King who has
known such 'intimacy' with God, a 'oneness' rendering all other experiences secondary and lacking, it will be difficult not to 'lust' after such
'oneness' again, like a lover who yearns for the company of the beloved.
And not just fellowship, but that rarest of 'intimate' liaisons, profound
encounters with the living God.

It is this 'spiritual lust' crippling and blinding the disciples in those early
days without Jesus, unable to imagine life without the physical presence
of Jesus, life without the intimacy of walking and talking with Him by the
seashore, the intimacy of knowing they were part of an inner circle, a
limited few, knowing Jesus like no other. They had yet to discover a 'new'
intimacy with Jesus, an intimacy Jesus describes as seeing Him in the life
of the 'other', an 'other' who looks nothing like Jesus, who takes rather
than gives, needing to be served rather than serve, offering no clues to
the 'presence of the Living Christ' lurking and hidden in the 'essence of
the other' (Matthew 25:40).

For those who have tasted that rarest of 'intimacies with Christ', 'lust'
will have to be kept at bay, redirected to a new way of 'knowing' and
experiencing intimacy with Christ, the intimacy of knowing and serving
the 'other'. Knowing Jesus in the encounters with the 'other' will not come
naturally. It too is 'late arriving' in the life of one trekking after God. But
be of good cheer, for knowing Jesus in the most intimate of ways will
come again, unexpectedly, 'like a thief in the night', in the moment when
you have not 'lusted', when you were not expecting, and suddenly you
'know Him'; "and their eyes were opened, and they recognized Him. And
He vanished from their sight" (Luke 24:31).

Day 39
ARE YOU CHAINED?

Now may the God of peace Himself sanctify you completely...
(1 Thessalonians 5:23)

"It will cost an intense narrowing of all our interests on earth, and an immense broadening of all our interests in God... Sanctification means intense concentration on God's point of view. It means every power of body, soul and spirit chained and kept for God's purpose only."– Oswald Chambers

The child trekking after the King has, no doubt, learned to 'concentrate on God's point of view', else they would have long ago ceased following, for God moves steadily and swiftly, and only those who have learned to 'concentrate' will succeed in 'staying on God's trail'. But 'concentrating' and 'chained' are two very different realities. The first, the intense concentration and consecration, is a gargantuan effort by the one trekking after God. No child can 'chain' their essence to the purposes of God. You can try, holding on tightfisted, but sooner or later your grip will relax and God will slip into the darkness.

The one who has been 'chained' to the very purposes of God knows those 'chains' are not the by-product of personal efforts; to the contrary, they are the response of God to a heart that has been 'completely and fully' consecrated unto God. Therein lies the danger. The child who has been 'chained' to the purposes of the King will soon discover a 'life' chained to God goes where God goes, when God goes. Chains easily create a very uncomfortable 'life condition'.

Indeed, the 'child so chained' will soon discover an "intense narrowing of all our interests on earth," but it will not matter, for the "interests in God" will aggressively fill the void created by an ever-increasing lack of attention toward earthly interests. Be warned, any attempt to force this narrowing of interests onto others will become a 'stifling legalism' to those forced to live within the confines of your 'chained existence'. Never assume your life-giving 'chains' will do anything but stifle and crush the spirit of those whom God has not set free by the shackling of 'life-giving chains'.

Day 40
FEED MY SHEEP

The Lord is the everlasting God, the Creator of the ends of the earth. He does not faint or grow weary...
(Isaiah 40:28)

"The process of being made broken bread and poured-out wine means that you have to be the nourishment for other souls until they learn to feed on God. They must drain you to the dregs. Be careful that you get your supply, or before long you will be utterly exhausted. Before other souls learn to draw on the life of the Lord Jesus direct, they have to draw on it through you; you have to be literally 'sucked', until they learn to take their nourishment from God."– Oswald Chambers

No child of the King, including Peter, has any concept of what 'feeding my sheep' will exact from them over the years of trekking after the Serving King. Hearing the tales of exhaustion from others will do little to prepare you for the toll 'feeding my sheep' will take upon your life. The trail is littered with the casualties of those who have fallen by the way-side utterly exhausted and spent, having attempted to feed others while not being fed.

Pausing to be fed is extremely problematic for a generation of followers who have long feasted on fast food, prepared to be devoured on the go, consumed while engaged in a myriad of activities. Rarely does God provide nourishment on the fly or even in the gathering of the many; instead, dining with God is almost always a solitary affair. You will be tempted to consume the appetizer, that gathering with the 'saints' in praise and worship over and over again. However, you cannot find the sustenance needed to 'feed my sheep' while in the frenzy of the many, delightful as that menu may be; no, the sustenance needed to 'feed my sheep' can only be found in solitary dining with the living God.

You will need to be mindful of the needed frequency of those solitary moments with God. Those who often feed the many need to be especially sensitive to refueling, taking in more than you are giving out. Resist the temptation to bask in the 'feeding of others', a constant threat. Find those needed moments to dine alone in the presence of the 'living God'. The road, littered with casualties, has too many victims already. When was your last meal?

Day 41
THE PICTURE

Lift up your eyes on high and see, Who created these?
(Isaiah 40:26)

"Nature to a saint is sacramental."– Oswald Chambers

Often those trekking after the Serving King develop a limiting and even debilitating habit of looking at the Word, and Word only, to see God. The 'Word' proclaims so much of what can be seen and known of God. But Word cannot say it all; instead, only in the glory of the creation can the 'unspoken' be seen and understood. You will have to stop walking, pause, look 'on high' and 'see' the glory of what God has created.

The danger of the 'sacrament of creation', like all sacraments, is that it can become too commonplace, too mundane, just part of the 'everyday' experience, and the very essence of 'sacrament' slips away into the abyss of 'normal and expected'. The sun, rising every morning, soon no longer surprises and delights the watchful eye. It is just too dependable, too 'everydayish' to elicit a response from those who 'see it', but in 'seeing' soon learn to 'see nothing' of the magnificent Creator; rather just the sun rising, as it always does, day after day. And, sacrament is gone, often forever, in the life of a child trekking after God.

So the risk of incarnation, God becoming 'flesh', an ordinary man among men. Soon, Jesus is no longer 'God in the flesh', with all the wonder and awe 'Godness' brings; but rather, simply Jesus, the man, the ordinary, just another piece of the dependable creation.

Remember to 'lift up your eyes and see' what only the eyes of a child of God can see. It will not happen with a 'glance'. No, you will have to 'stop', really 'stop', and 'look up' with 'eyes' that can 'see', 'eyes' that have been trained to discern the hand of God in the sacrament of creation, in the mundane of the utterly unbelievable moments found in experiencing the creation. Be not surprised when in that moment of 'seeing', the God Who created speaks boldly into the heart and mind of the one who has 'stopped' and 'looked up'.

Day 42

CAN YOU STILL IMAGINE?

You keep him in perfect peace whose mind is stayed on You, because he trusts in You.
(Isaiah 26:3)

"Is your imagination stayed on God or is it starved? The starvation of the imagination is one of the most fruitful sources of exhaustion and sapping in a worker's life. If you have never used your imagination to put yourself before God, begin to do it now."– Oswald Chambers

'Imagination' for many trekking after God suggests a negative connotation, implying 'not real' or 'make pretend', rather than the crucial ability to 'hear' and 'see' God in the mundane and profane. You will have to 'grow up' and learn how to use your 'imagination' again, as powerfully as a child, if you are to succeed in 'seeing' and 'hearing' as Jesus called us to (Matthew 11:15). It is only the 'imagination' that will enable you to 'see and hear' the very essence of God, imprinted deep into the 'mind' of the 'seer', the one who can still 'imagine'.

This will not come easy for most, having lost the ability to 'imagine' our way into the very presence of the Living God. Ours is a culture of 'science', with its rigid and stifling rules, insisting only that which can be 'measured' and 'measured repeatedly' be given any attention. The ability to 'imagine' is forbidden, relegated to the land of make pretend, robbing the child of God of the Creator's tremendous gift to those who are willing to use it, explore it, embrace it, and allow 'imagination' to usher in reality and life in ways that the 'measurable' never can. So Chambers warns us of the dangers of a "starved imagination," weak and feeble, unable to usher us into the very presence of the 'Living God'.

Even in this godless land of the unimagined dominated by the demigods of science, the artists among us valiantly seek to keep the imagination alive, vibrant, capable of transcending the mundane of that which can be measured, ushering the child of God, into the very essence of God, into the very presence of the 'Living God'. 'Imagination' is that pathway, gifted by God, enabling all who are willing to explore it to find the very essence of the 'Living God'. You will have to shake off the mundane world of science to get there, but it can be done. "If you have never used your imagination to put yourself before God, begin to do it now."

Day 43
TELL THE PROPHET TO BE QUIET!

You speak to us, and we will listen; but do not let God speak to us, lest we die.
(Exodus 20:19)

"'Speak thou with us … but let not God speak with us.' We show how little we love God by preferring to listen to His servants only. We like to listen to personal testimonies, but we do not desire that God Himself should speak to us. Why are we so terrified lest God should speak to us?"– Oswald Chambers

How is it possible that a God who speaks so often, with so much detail, so much precision, with particulars designed especially for the intended recipient, is so rarely heard by those who claim to be God's children? You will be tempted to proclaim, "God is no longer speaking!", but nothing could be further from the truth. The God of Scripture 'babbles on endlessly' (Hebrews 1:1).

Still, you rest in the assurance having never uttered such words, such foolishness, words that hush the voice of God, mute God, render God passive and voiceless in your presence. Like those early trekkers, you have mastered the art of listening to the 'servants', those masters of proclamation, pontificating endlessly week after week, month after month, insulating you from the directives of the 'ever-present God' Who speaks directly to the heart of the listener. It is the modern prophet, the pastor, the 'professional' who provides the protection of 'speak Thou with us'.

So the genius of the modern trekker, under the guise of 'pastor speak to us', hiding in the noise of the 'prophet', rendered safe from the voice of the 'Living God'. The modern prophet, unlike those predecessors long ago, carries no more the 'voice of God' moniker. The modern prophet, just another voice amongst the many to be ignored or debated, hidden in, avoiding the only voice that matters, the only voice that cannot be debated, cannot be avoided, the 'Voice' demanding obedience 'lest we die'.

Rebuke the terror of the many. You have nothing to fear. Let the voice of God ring clearly into your being. Tell the 'modern prophet', "Shssssh, I am listening to God." Then those trekking after God will gather, not to hear God, but to tell the stories of what God has said.

Day 44
SILENCING THE WANTS

Speak, for Your servant hears.
(1 Samuel 3:10)

"Because I have listened definitely to one thing from God, it does not follow that I will listen to everything He says...If I have not cultivated this devotion of hearing, I can only hear God's voice at certain times; at other times I am taken up with things–things which I say I must do, and I become deaf to Him, I am not living the life of a child."–Oswald Chambers

It is not uncommon for the child of God to proclaim, "I heard God." But having heard and hearing are vastly different realities. The former, 'heard God', is a vital part of spiritual formation; but, it is only the 'foundation' of the work God has yet to do. You will be tempted, immensely tempted, to live on that foundation, building your own home, carefully crafted to your precise dimensions, resting peacefully on the foundation of what you have 'heard'. However, that is not what God intended.

True, God builds an amazing foundation for the child trekking after Him, and it will indeed support a great number of houses built by our own specifications, but God's intent is to never stop with the 'foundation', rather to continue building a 'house' fashioned by the specifications of the King.

You will be tempted to say, "I must have this room" or "This is the color I want," and hearing no objection from the Designer, you will assume the Designer's silence is tacit approval. Only later do you discover the Designer was not silent; rather, "I have not cultivated this devotion of hearing" for it is our desires and wants that render us deaf to the voice of the Living Designer. The noise of our 'desires and wants' presents an endless chattering and clamoring of 'white noise' rendering the voice of the Designer muted, distant, too faint to 'hear'. You will have to stop, close your eyes, demand your 'wants and desires' to hush, to stop clamoring long enough for you to hear the voice of the Designer.

Understand your 'wants and desires' are never foolish in the deafening of your being. They will simply start whispering, every so softly, building toward a crescendo rendering you deaf, a deafness so slow in arriving, you will never notice its crippling effect as you trek after the suddenly quiet Designer.

Day 45
A MOMENT OF DARKNESS

So have no fear of them, for nothing is covered that will not be revealed, or hidden that will not be known. What I tell you in the dark, say in the light, and what you hear whispered, proclaim on the housetops.
(Matthew 10:27)

"Are you in the dark just now in your circumstances, or in your life with God? Then remain quiet. If you open your mouth in the dark, you will talk in the wrong mood: darkness is the time to listen. Don't talk to other people about it; don't read books to find out the reason of the darkness, but listen and heed. If you talk to other people, you cannot hear what God is saying." – Oswald Chambers

Learning to hear God, the 'whispering God', is a learned art, and it is fraught with the trauma of knowing you have 'heard' from the Living God, as the two of you dine in the 'dark'. The 'fear' of which Jesus speaks, the 'fear' of knowing what the Father has 'whispered', specifics for life, leaving little room for disobedience, renders you 'fearful' of how others will react to your proclamation, those simple words, "Jesus whispered to me."

How odd it is that the proclamation that is to be 'proclaimed' from the housetops has no bearing for the 'life of the other', but, rather, is a clear directive for God's dinner guest only, that courageous one who has paused from the 'urgency of the important', the 'tyranny of the ought', to dine with the 'ever-present God', in the solitude of darkness God mandates for those who dine in His presence. The proclamation is about how 'being and life' have been directed by the Living God toward the child dining with God, and that child alone. Why does the child feel threatened by proclaiming the 'whispers' of the Living God?

The ability to hear God, the 'whispering God', unsettles the 'many' who have heard no 'whispering' from God, no directives, no particulars regarding this or that, no 'you must do this or that'; instead, theirs is a silent dinner in the 'dark', void of the ever-present God. And they will not be happy God has chosen to 'whisper' to the child of God proclaiming on the housetop. But, of course, God has no favorites, no special children, no 'by invitation only'; rather, God 'proclaims' from the housetop, "Come and dine." Few are those who enter the 'darkness' to hear the 'whispering God'. If you are one of the few, 'have no fear of them...and proclaim on the housetops'.

Day 46

THE OTHER'S HAND

**For none of us lives to himself, and none of us dies to himself.
(Romans 14:7)**

"'Whether one member suffer, all the members suffer with it.' When once you allow physical selfishness, mental slovenliness, moral obtuseness, spiritual density, everyone belonging to your crowd will suffer."–Oswald Chambers

Ours is an isolated world, a world in which life as community is just a distant memory, barely visible in that moment of reflection, a world of fences and garages making it difficult to imagine a world where the suffering of the 'one' becomes the suffering of the 'all'. Communal suffering is a distant concept for most. But the Body of Christ, the Church, is a remnant of our communal history, a distant time when 'all things were held in common'.

Communal suffering in the Body of Christ is not like the suffering we experience with our bodies. A stubbed toe, broken and ragged, sends an immediate message of pain to the rest of the body, hopping around howling as the pain rages through every fiber of the human body. However, the Body of Christ with its autonomous members living in proximity, but disconnected, safely sealed away in protective cocoons, does not experience the direct pain of the 'other'. Thus, 'the wounded member' simply cries out into the night, isolated, alone in the crowd of the many, wondering why the 'others' have not come to assist, to offer healing and grace.

For the child trekking after the King, a new reality, a new presence slowly begins to emerge along the path. It is the 'other', likewise following the King, yearning to 'be and do' just as the King commands. Then it dawns on you, and you wonder how you could have missed it for so very long, grab the hand of the 'other' who has suddenly been there all along.

Be warned as you reach out to embrace the 'hand' of the 'other'. That 'hand' will bring you great joy, and pain, and celebration, and despair, and you will soon realize every follower has two hands. And the 'other' knows another 'other', who knows another 'other', who knows another 'other', and so on. Then that moment of clarity arrives, "everyone belonging to your crowd will suffer." Dare you grab the hand of the other as you trek on after the Serving King.

Day 47
RESURRECTION

**Awake, O sleeper, and arise from the dead, and Christ will shine
on you.
(Ephesians 5:14)**

*"When the inspiration of God does come, it comes with such
miraculous power that we are able to arise from the dead and
do the impossible thing. The remarkable thing about spiritual initiative is that the life comes after we do the 'bucking
up.'"–Oswald Chambers*

Admittedly, it is a difficult thing to realize you have been 'sleeping with
your eyes wide open'. Still more difficult is the realization you are 'dead',
lifeless, incapable of 'being and doing' what you were intended to 'be and
do'; yet, all the while you have been 'being and doing' as only the 'dead'
can 'be and do'. That takes a moment to 'get your head around'. You
will be tempted to say, "I'm walking and talking, how can I be dead?" Or
worse yet, "I'm walking and talking with Jesus, surely I am alive and well!"

Then, in that moment of 'quiet solitude in the dark' with God, the fullness of what you can 'be and do' begins to emerge as the voice of God
throws life-giving light into the abandoned recesses of your life. Suddenly,
dreams of hopefulness long given up as dead, lying deep within your
being, hidden from the grace of God Whose power waits to resurrect
those lifeless dimensions of your being, begin to appear on the horizon
of your mind.

However, you will have to 'arise' on your own initiative in the newfound power God has spoken into the dead recesses of your being. The
'dead' has atrophied, unused for such a very long time. Then a small
quiver, a pulse of vitality, alive again, but like all resurrections, it must
learn to crawl again, walk again, run again. The previously dead must
find strength and vitality in the being of God.

Suddenly and unexpectedly, as the once 'dead' begins to 'be and do',
light suddenly begins to fall upon more and more of your being, ushering
in 'life' and 'vitality' to the once 'dead', and even the yet 'still dead' longing
for the 'light' of God to find it as well. With each newly resurrected aspect
of your being comes the awareness that there is so much 'dead' left to
be resurrected. But hope has returned.

Day 48
NO TIME FOR PITY

**"It is enough; now, O Lord, take away my life, for I am no better than my fathers." And Elijah lay down and slept under a broom tree. And behold, an angel touched him and said to him, "Arise and eat."
(1 Kings 19:5)**

"The angel did not give Elijah a vision, or explain the Scriptures to him, or do anything remarkable; he told Elijah to do the most ordinary thing, viz., to get up and eat."– Oswald Chambers

The resurrected life, that 'awakening of the dead', the 'trek after the Living God', is a long protracted journey, a journey fraught with frailty and failure. The conscientious child of God will, from time to time, sit down with Elijah and say, "It is enough now, O Lord, take away my life for I am no better that my fathers." Indeed, in some sense, the child of God is no better than the 'fathers' who have attempted to trek after God before them.

God will have nothing of your moment of pity, focused on self-accomplishment or the lack thereof. Nor will God run to your rescue with some vision of grandeur, lifting you to visions yet unknown, but soon to come. No, more times than not, God's gracious intervention is to remind you to 'eat'. The simple affirmation will take some getting used to as you trek after the King. It is in the mundane, the unextraordinary, the run-of-the-mill, in which most of life after the King is spent.

The invitation to eat, rest and catch your breath is the simplest grace of all as God does not chasten you for your 'pity party', nor for the 'failures' that ushered in the 'pity party'; rather, the King simply dines with you, refreshing you for the journey awaiting the child trekking after the King. Remember, as you eat in silence, the King does not slumber, nor does the King tarry days on end. There are great journeys laying ahead for the one who has eaten their way out of pity. "And Elijah arose and ate and drank, and went in the strength of that food forty days and forty nights to Horeb, the mount of God" (1 Kings 19:7-8). Eat and drink, for there is plenty of journey left ahead.

Day 49
THIS TOO IS FORGIVEN

"Rise, let us be going..."
(Matthew 26:46)

"The sense of the irreparable is apt to make us despair, and we say– 'It is all up now, it is no use trying anymore.' If we imagine that this kind of despair is exceptional, we are mistaken, it is a very ordinary human experience...Never let the sense of failure corrupt your new action."– Oswald Chambers

Sadly, it is inevitable at some point along the journey you will fall asleep, as exhaustion, an ever-present companion of the child trekking after the King, renders you helpless against the 'rest' lurking in wait. Don't be surprised when it seizes you at the moment when Jesus most relies on you. However, you must remember that when Jesus relies on you, it is not a make or break proposition. Nothing in the Kingdom of God is left solely dependent on the feeble efforts of those trekking after the King.

Nor will your 'sleepiness' render you 'finished' as a follower of the King. No, even in that critical moment, the moment in which you have opportunity to shine, to rise up and 'be' all that you can be, the grace of Jesus covers a multitude of missed opportunities. So, He wakes the slumbering child of the King and offers the simple, "Rise, let us be going..."

The fatigue of failure is a drowsiness that is difficult to shake off. Failure, especially failure in a critical moment, sticks to the back of the child of God in a way that only grace can 'shake'. You will be tempted to sit down and rest again long before the next leg of the journey is over. But you must not go to sleep again, for the 'eyes were heavy' will occur yet again, and with each sleep cycle, the weight of failure drags the eyes deeper and deeper into the slumber of hopelessness.

Yet, even in that deep slumber, that third slumber of failure in that critical moment, you will hear His voice calling you to "Rise, let us be going," and you must shake the fatigue of failure, for it is Jesus calling you once again to rise and 'be going' with Him. If you will allow Him to do so, He will free you from the heavy load of 'failure' you carry. Indeed, "Never let your sense of failure corrupt your new action." Trek on after the Serving King.

Day 50
DRUDGERY OF A CERTAIN KIND

Arise, shine, for your light has come...
(Isaiah 60:1)

"We must do the thing and not lie like a log. If we will arise and shine, drudgery becomes divinely transfigured. Drudgery is one of the finest touchstones of character there is."– Oswald Chambers

It will not take long into the journey of 'trekking after God' to discover the King rarely engages in the activity of royalty, reclining at the banquet table; but rather, is about the drudgery of 'washing the feet of fishermen' (John 13) before the banquet begins. Worse yet, the King will soon turn toward you and insist on performing such drudgery upon you, tempting you to join Peter in proclaiming, "You shall never wash my feet!" You, too, will have to learn the humility necessary for the King to teach you by His servitude toward you.

You will be tempted yet again to say, "That task is just too lowly for Jesus to engage in toward me." But that is not really the reason for the vigorous objection. For you have let Him serve you countless times before in ways that seemed more suitable to you. No, it is those fateful words you know are forthcoming in which the way of Jesus becomes the mandate for the child trekking after the King. "For I have given you an example, that you also ought to wash one another's feet" (John 13:15).

Now, you are 'front and center', nowhere to hide, no excuse, no pleas of "I don't know how!" You are profoundly stuck, trapped in the example exacted upon you, as the Serving King washed your feet, in spite of all your pleas to resist. Then you hear it, "Arise and shine, for your light has come." Your moment of 'drudgery' has arrived, it is time to kneel, grab the 'towel and basin' and shine in that way only a true child of the King can shine. No, not sitting at the banquet table while the world clamors to serve you; rather, 'washing the feet' of those whom you will later have the privilege of serving.

And yes, they will not be the 'kings and queens' of the world; rather, just the simple 'fishermen' whom Jesus has called to the banquet, who have leaped at the chance to be served by the King at the glorious banquet called in their honor. Then it dawns on you, startling you, blinding you. You suddenly realize your light has come.

Day 51
THE DANGER OF DAYDREAMING

Rise, let us go from here.
(John 14:31)

"If you are in love, you do not sit down and 'dream' about the one you love all the time, you go and do something for him; and that is what Jesus Christ expects us to do."– Oswald Chambers

The philosopher knows a 'real' thing is preeminently better than the 'idea' of a thing. Likewise, in the Kingdom of God 'being and doing' are far superior to the 'dream of being and doing'. Nonetheless, daydreaming requires little effort and no consequences, so we think, and, therefore, we are ever tempted to live in the world of 'daydreaming'.

Slothfulness has consequences of its own, a slow rendering of the dreamer into a state of lethargy, slowly and consistently nibbling away at the vitality and viability of the dreamer to 'be and do'. The dreamers, the ones who have mastered the art of thinking about 'being and doing', will not notice the loss. Instead, they have learned to find contentment, a dangerous fulfillment while dwelling in a 'world of ideas' in which 'being and doing' is painlessly executed in the 'world of ideas' morphing into the dreamer's every whim, creating the wonderful illusion of 'being and doing' in a world that doesn't exist.

It is in those moments of peaceful bliss that the 'dreamer' discovers even the 'idea of Jesus' will not remain under the dreamer's authority, as even the 'idea of Jesus' refuses to be a mere pawn in the dreamer's fantasy. Even in the daydream, Jesus "expects us to do," even there He commands the dreamer to "rise, let us go from here." He is relentless in His pursuit of even the dreamer, quick to remind the dreamer to 'get up' and 'go'.

Then the dreamer must awake, must rise and go, must 'be and do' in pursuit of the 'real' Jesus, or run the risk of falling even deeper into the blissful 'world of ideas'. It is time "let us go from here." Trek on...

Day 52

JUST FOR THE GLORY OF GOD

**"Why was the oil wasted like that?"..."Leave her alone. Why do you trouble her? She has done a beautiful thing to Me."
(Mark 14:6)**

"We have to get rid of this notion– 'Am I of any use?' and make up our minds that we are not, and we may be near the truth. It is never a question of being of use, but of being of value to God Himself. When we are abandoned to God, He works through us all the time."– Oswald Chambers

It is a humbling thing to understand God does not 'need' you or the gifts you bring. God is quite capable of 'caring for the poor among us' without our gifts of charity, well intentioned as they may be. More humbling is the realization that 'caring for the poor among us' is not your primary function in serving the Living God. It is an awkward moment when Jesus scolds you for scolding those who want to lavishly give to God in ways you deem an inappropriate use of the resources God has provided.

Moderns take great delight in chastising the Church for its 'ridiculous' expressions of gratitude toward God in both art and architecture, so much so that communities of faith have retreated into art and architecture reflecting the mundane rather than the glorious expressions of gratitude that rose to the skies in the cathedrals of a bygone era.

But for those who have stood in awe, straining upward to see the intricate majesty of the Sistine Chapel, or marveling at the mosaics of St. Peter's Basilica, or stood in rhapsody as the organ bellowed at St. Paul's, such outpourings of 'oil' can do no other than to soothe the very being of God, Who basks in the 'beautiful thing' offered to God, and to God alone. For the child busy with serving, when was the last time you lavished God with the foolishness of beauty, the outlandish gift of 'oil', the majesty of...?

'Leave them alone' for it is a beautiful thing to God, as we pause from our trek and lavish God with an abundance of 'oil'. The Serving King is not offended by that "beautiful thing to me." Pause from the grandeur of serving, pour oil on the feet of the Serving King.

Day 53
HAVE YOU EVER BEEN STILL?

Be still, and know that I am God...

(Psalm 46:10)

"One of the greatest strains in life is the strain of waiting for God."– Oswald Chambers

For the child trekking fervently after God, the command to simply 'be still' seems harsh, bordering on unrealistic, especially in a world with so much needing to be done. Therein lies the problem, learning the difference between 'what only God can do' and 'what we are to do'. Early in the journey, the child of God lives in the illusion of their 'doing', taking great pride in the accomplishments of 'doing'. Be warned, 'doing', illusionary as it may be, brings great rewards to one's sense of 'well-being' through accomplishment.

It will not be until much later in the journey when the task ahead is beyond the reach of what the child can do that the child of God senses the need to 'stop trying'; instead, "Be still and know that I am God." As 'stillness' becomes reality, another world begins to appear on the horizon, a world that has been there all along, a world in which the hand of God is at work in ways that could not have been seen by a moving 'eye', a world invisible to the 'eye' that is not 'still'. But in the stillness of non-movement for body, mind and soul, a stillness more profound than the child of God has ever known, a stillness only found in utter and complete 'non-doing', God appears, materializing as if from nowhere, engaged in the business of 'upholding the creation' with His Word (Hebrews 1:3).

A new understanding begins to embrace the mind of the child of God who has finally discovered 'stillness' before God. It has been God Who has been 'doing' all the while.

A new, even profound, humbleness descends into the very being of the child of God, realizing for the first time in the midst of a stillness of mind, body and soul, that all of their 'doing' has not been 'their doing' at all; instead, it has been God all along, Who in the mandated 'stillness' so very few discover, allows the child of God to 'see' what has been happening all along; God at work. "Be still, very still, and know that I am God." A very different kind of trekking on.

Day 54

HAVE YOU SEEN THE SMILE?

...the Son of Man came not to be served but to serve, and to give His life as a ransom for many.
Matthew 20:28

"The mainspring of Paul's service is not love for men, but love for Jesus Christ. If we are devoted to the cause of humanity, we shall soon be crushed and broken-hearted, for we shall often meet with more ingratitude from men than we would from a dog; but if our motive is love to God, no ingratitude can hinder us from serving our fellow men."– Oswald Chambers

No amount of platitudes can change the reality of 'servanthood' and the toll it takes on the occupational servant, that child of the King, trekking along in service to Him Who serves. Further, in a culture of 'entitlements', sometimes found even in the church, with the cultural expectation of 'service' and 'opportunity', especially from those identified as 'servants of the King', gratefulness can be long and hard to come by; at least, a gratefulness bringing about actual change in the life of the one being served. Sadly, "we shall often meet with more ingratitude from men than we would from a dog." That, of course, leads to the question of 'why'? Why would anyone continue to serve in the midst of such ingratitude?

The question is a warning, reasonable and sincere as it may be, to all those contemplating the journey of trekking after the King: motivation is everything, and only one motivation, love for the 'Serving King', will keep you engaged in the process of serving the so-called 'mongrels' gathering in the King's banquet halls scattered across the land. Still, you will wonder, why does He 'give His life as a ransom for many'?

Then, in that moment least expected, that rarest of occasions, a mongrel speaks the simplest of words, words that empower and renew, words that bring life to both servant and the one being served, words bringing a smile to the face of the King, "Thank you." Then, and only then, comes that moment of understanding. It is not the 'thank you' that empowers and ushers forth life. No, rather, it is the 'smile' of the King.

Day 55
ARE YOU GLAD?

"I will most gladly spend and be spent for you."
(2 Corinthians 12:15)

"We have no right in Christian work to be guided by our affinities; this is one of the biggest tests of our relationship to Jesus Christ."– Oswald Chambers

For the child trekking after the King, the privilege of 'affinities' is a difficult thing to surrender. Life, until the moment of 'calling', has been spent chasing 'affinities' of every kind. But the King, nor the King's Son, will allow any 'affinity' to rival one's devotion to the Lordship of Christ. This devotion to Jesus is a devotion of a special kind, a devotion directed not simply to Jesus Himself, but to the 'interests' of Jesus. That is the 'biggest test' awaiting the child trekking after the King.

Being 'spent' for Jesus is profoundly different from being 'spent' for the 'cause' of Jesus, or so you will be tempted to believe. In reality, they are one and the same, and it is the recognition of that 'sameness' that ushers in the possibility of 'most gladly' arriving in the emotional being of the child trekking after God. You must take seriously, more seriously than you have imagined, the reality of 'being spent', especially as you trek after the 'Serving King'.

When the recognition of 'being spent' begins to noticeably impact well-being, when the theory of 'being spent' transitions to actuality, the necessity of 'loving' who and what Jesus loves becomes critical to sustaining your trek after the 'being spent' King. For it is in those moments of 'being spent' one suddenly realizes the absence of the ever- present Jesus. That 'absence' of the 'ever-present' Jesus ushers in a crisis of immense proportion for the child who does not understand 'loving what Jesus loves' is synonymous with loving the 'ever-present' Jesus.

At stake is not the reality of being 'spent', for you cannot trek after the Serving King without being spent. 'Spentness' is the price of trekking after the Serving King; instead, the issue is simply one of 'gladly', that is, are you 'gladly' being spent in your service to 'who' and 'what' Jesus loves? Dare you trek on?

Day 56
A LIFE SPENT FOR WHAT?

If I love you more, am I to be loved less?
(2 Corinthians 12:15)

"The real test of the saint is not preaching the gospel, but washing disciples' feet, that is, doing the things that do not count in the actual estimate of men, but count everything in the estimate of God." – Oswald Chambers

The death of the expectation to be 'loved', or at least appreciated, by those for whom life has been 'spent' loving is an 'expectation' that dies slowly in the life of a child trekking after the 'Serving King'. This is never more truer than in the life of one who has been 'spent' doing the 'unvalued' acts of service the Serving King often mandates. It is the 'things that do not count' that will threaten the survival of the child trekking after the King, for the child will have a profound sense that a 'life spent' doing 'things that do not count' cannot have value. And that is a profound problem for the child of God. Life that is 'spent' ought to have 'value', but to 'whom' is the question?

You will spend immense amounts of energy attempting to add 'value' to your efforts; that is, to have others value your efforts in service to the King. To that end, you will call the culture around to 'value' service to the poor, aid to the crippled, hand-ups toward the drunken and drugged, etc. But in the end, you know, in spite of all the effort and resources that have been garnered for your cause, the culture, even the culture of the Church, may not 'value' that which God deems so valuable, even worth dying for.

Eventually, you will be forced into that dialogue with the 'Serving King', a dialogue challenging the 'Serving King', beckoning God to explain why loving those who will ultimately not 'love back' has such value in the heart of God? You will want to hear, "Because some of those you have loved will indeed love back." But slowly, ever so slowly, the child trekking after the 'Serving King' begins to realize what God 'values' is a 'life spent' without concern for consequence, productivity, or pragmatism; a 'life spent' simply for the sake of love, love for the 'Serving King'. The lack of pragmatism by God will truly grate your spirit, until you have learned to love as the Son has loved.

Day 57
HOW CAN HE?

**"The woman said to Him, 'Sir, You have nothing
to draw water with...'"
(John 4:11)**

*"My misgivings arise from the fact that I ransack my own
person to find out how He will be able to do it. My questions spring from the depths of my own inferiority. If I detect
these misgivings in myself, let me bring them to the light
and confess them— 'Lord, I have had misgivings about Thee,
I have not believed in Thy wits apart from my own; I have
not believed in Thine Almighty power apart from my finite
understanding of it.'"– Oswald Chambers*

The 'unspent' child of God lives in the illusion of having something to offer the 'Serving King' and that is problematic, immensely problematic, but the condition of all who attempt to trek after the 'Serving King'. Thus, they will be confused by the commands of the King to do that which is beyond one's bag of current resources. More tragic, the 'unspent' child will assume 'doing' is limited to the resources in the hands of the child. That evaluation process will carryover concerning the King as well, "Sir, you have nothing to draw water with," for you confuse the King's abilities with your own, a dangerous confusion for all followers.

That, of course, explains the ultimate necessity of being spent, to discover what can be done long after the child of the King has 'spent' all, every smidgen, every diminutive speck of resource the child of the King can muster. Therein lies the stumbling block, the kink, the restriction, to 'life abundant'. The child of the King will continue to approach life and ministry based upon the 'in-hand' resources of the child, and never discover the joy of a life dependent upon the 'unseen bucket' of the King.

So few will find this 'spentness' ushering in utter dependence upon the 'Serving King'. Even the few who do will struggle to move forward in obedience, when the 'bucketless King' gives direction for life and ministry. Of course, that is precisely the point. The Serving King is never lacking. Resist the temptation to ask Him, "where will You get living water?" Resources are the problem of the King. Yours is simply to trek on in obedience.

Day 58
LIVING WATER

"Where do You get that living water?"
(John 4:11)

"When we get into difficult circumstances, we impoverish His ministry by saying– 'Of course He cannot do any thing,' and we struggle down to the deeps and try to get the water for ourselves. Beware of the satisfaction of sinking back and saying– 'It can't be done'; you know it can be done if you look to Jesus."– Oswald Chambers

Contentment in 'spentness' is a dangerous unintended consequence for the child of the King who has been authentically 'spent'. You will be tempted to delight in 'spentness' and to bask in the contentment of having been 'poured out'. But 'broken' and 'poured out' is not meant as a final state; rather, the condition out of which 'significance' can now rise to the surface. Still, 'significance' will not come without pursuing this 'living water' of which Jesus speaks. And pursue it you must.

Understand the great temptation, lurking in the subtleties of the mind, the road taken by far too many who have given much to the Serving King, to simply sit back at the end of a long season of 'spentness', and proclaim, "It can't be done" and "I have nothing left to give." And, more to the point, "I have earned this season of 'spentness', a time to rest in doing nothing." But it is this condition of 'spentness', so critical in preparing the child of the King for the 'living water' and its life-giving propensity for those who drink deeply and consistently, which draws one to the 'living water'.

However, the child trekking after the Serving King must resist the temptation to return to the 'water' that cannot quench the thirst of the spent traveler. It is that 'old water' that has been spent and no infusion of 'old water' can provide the vitality and purpose God intends. Only 'living water' can meet the need of the truly 'spent'. It is 'living water' that renews and empowers for a 'life' of 'spentness' intended for His followers. So we join her in asking, "Where do you get that living water?" It can only be found in the Person of Jesus. Drink deeply. The trek is far too long to attempt without it. Drink and trek on.

Day 59
COMMON SENSE

"...this is why we believe that You came from God." Jesus answered them, "Do you now believe?"
John 16:30-31

The soul has got out of intimate contact with God by leaning to its own religious understanding. There is no sin in it, and no punishment attached to it; but when the soul realizes how he has hindered his understanding of Jesus Christ, and produced for himself perplexities and sorrows and difficulties, it is with shame and contrition he has to come back.—Oswald Chambers

The danger of remembering the Words of Jesus, without knowing the Christ who spoke them, cannot be overstated. Following the illusive 'Serving King' requires rigorous attention, careful tracking, a hypersensitivity to the movement of the 'Spirit of God'. But 'codified words', or 'law', are so much easier to access and use in a 'common sense' kind of way, which is precisely the problem. A 'common sense' approach to the Words of Christ will not reveal the 'Truth' God intends, otherwise the Spirit would be unnecessary. Clearly, this is no small matter. So the great temptation for the child trekking after the 'Serving King', the 'itch' to use 'common sense', rather than rely on the inspiration of the 'resurrected Christ' to provide meaning and depth. Common sense is so much easier a road to follow than 'revelation'.

Paul warned the child of God only the 'spiritual mind' can comprehend the things of the Spirit (Romans 8:6) and those who seek a 'common sense' approach will end up seeing only what 'flesh' can reveal. It is this shallowness of depth and insight that renders the disciples vulnerable to being 'scattered, each to his own home' (John 16:32). Thus, you will have to decide early on to never approach the 'Word' without 'knowing Jesus', never to be confused with 'knew Him'. It is the intimacy with Christ that empowers the eyes to 'see' what 'common sense' can never comprehend. Yes, you must look deeper into the 'Word' than common sense dictates, for only in that deep look, that deep gulp, can 'living water' be found.

Be not surprised when you 'know Him', and 'common sense' simply cannot process what only Spirit can know. You will, from time to time, have to leave your old trusted friend, common sense, behind. And, yes, He will ask, "Do you now believe?"

Day 60

HAVE YOU CREATED A DISTURBANCE?

And he cried out, "Jesus, Son of David, have mercy on me!" And those who were in front rebuked him, telling him to be silent. But he cried out all the more. "What do you want Me to do for you?" Jesus said. "Lord, let me recover my sight." (Luke 18:38-41)

"Persist in the disturbance until you yet get face to face with the Lord Himself; do not deify common sense. When Jesus asks us what we want Him to do for us in regard to the incredible thing with which we are faced, remember that He does not work in common sense ways, but in supernatural ways."
– Oswald Chambers

For the child trekking after the King, 'common sense', especially 'common sense' rooted in recent personal experience and the testimony of the 'crowd', will be exceptionally difficult to throw off. 'Common sense' shackles the child of God to 'life in the flesh' and you will be hard pressed to break free from the limitations of 'common sense'. But be warned, even if you should break free from the 'common sense' shackling mind and spirit, the 'crowd' will not be pleased with your newfound confidence in the Christ.

Even the 'crowd' of the Church may 'rebuke' you and demand that you be silent as Jesus walks by with you in tow; and that is the ultimate irony, as the One Who unshackles from 'common sense' becomes the reason for silencing the child of the King recklessly 'trekking after the King' in the most 'uncommonsensical' way. Then, and only then, you must decide whether or not to create that 'disturbance' that does, indeed, disturb.

However, understand 'common sense' will never go quietly into the night, even long after it has been shown to be the 'fool' over and over again. 'Common sense' will 'dog you', hound you back into submission. Should you resist the pull of 'common sense' to return to normal, it will beckon unto the ever-willing crowd to assist in silencing you, rendering you 'common' once again, just like everyone else in a crowd that long ago stopped making a 'disturbance'. And yet, you hear Him, "What do you want Me to do?" Dare you create a 'disturbance'?

Day 61

HAVE YOU THE PRIVILEGE OF EXAMINATION?

He said to him the third time, "Simon, son of John, do you love Me?" Peter was grieved because He said to him the third time, "Do you love Me?
(John 21:17)

"The word of the Lord pierces even to the dividing asunder of soul and spirit, there is no deception left. There is no possibility of being sentimental with the Lord's question; you cannot say nice things when the Lord speaks directly to you, the hurt is too terrific. It is such a hurt that it stings every other concern out of account." – Oswald Chambers

It is no easy thing to be examined by the Son, especially in that probing way in which Jesus refuses to accept those 'pat answers' we have so beautifully and meaningfully prepared for the King, flowing from the 'sentimentality' of a relationship with Jesus. That is the 'hurtful' dimension, the fact that we have 'meant' every word, have considered carefully this response from the heart, only to hear the Son question yet again, that which has been so carefully expressed. For this child, trekking after the King is not new to the journey; rather, the privilege of this examination 'even to the dividing asunder of soul and spirit', and it is a privilege presented to the very few, comes only to the child who has kept pace with the Serving King for an extended period of time, years on end. This is an advanced examination few will ever face.

Thus, the 'grief', the sudden awareness that for all the 'trekking after God', for all the years spent 'right on His heals', the Son probes ever so deeply into a heart that thought it loved the Son completely, only to be challenged, pierced yet again, by this probing question from the Son Who seems to know what even the 'heart' has not known, 'love' is yet lacking. The grief can be overwhelming to the unprepared child, the child who seriously believed the work of transformation of the 'heart' was done.

But be of good cheer for the Son is not finished yet. His probing is not to indict, but rather to demonstrate there is still a 'work of the heart' yet to be done, yet to be completed, yet to 'be' all that 'love' can be. Be not dismayed long into the journey when the Son asks yet again, "Do you love me?" He is not condemning you; rather, He is preparing you for a transformation so profound that only the Son could know there is still liberating work yet to be done. Fear not. Trek on...

Day 62
THE ROAD LESS TRAVELLED

"Lord, You know everything; You know that I love you."
(John 21:17)

Peter was beginning to discover to himself how much he did love the Lord, that there was no one in heaven above or upon earth beneath beside Jesus Christ; but he did not know it until the probing, hurting questions of the Lord came.
– Oswald Chambers

It is an amazing moment, almost beyond words, when a desired 'state' becomes a 'reality'. Peter, in the midst of great grief, suddenly discovers a joy that only comes to those who know the joy of examination before the King. Joy is the fruit of 'passing' this examination from the Son. Oh, the joy of 'self-realization' confirming what we have dared to dream might be the case, an actual 'love' for Jesus, blossoming in the innermost being of the child trekking after the King.

But you cannot know that, really know it, until you have survived the 'hurt' that only Jesus can inflict upon the core of your being. The hurt caused by the others, that random group of family, friends and enemies who pierce the heart, intentionally and unintentionally, driving you into the arms of Jesus. However, that hurt can never help you to 'know' if you love Jesus. Only the hurt that comes directly from Jesus Himself can help you to know if you truly love Him as you hear Him ask, "Were they right about you?"

To know that 'hurt' which pierces the core of your being, you will first have to survive an ever-present and nagging question, "Does Jesus really love me?" We are not used to being 'hurt' by those who are supposed to love us. Ours is a culture of love and acceptance, "just as I am," and it cuts against the grain to think one who loves us deeply and profoundly would actually 'hurt' us. It is only after you 'know' the hurt from the Lover of your soul that you are free to know, to experience, a love for the One who 'hurts' you, Who cuts you to the very core of your being.

Then, the moment of insight, the transforming realization, the staggering truth, He was made "perfect through suffering" (Hebrews 2:10) and you suddenly discover you are on that final road, the road to perfection. The circle is complete. You know that He loves you.

Day 63
TENDING SHEEP

"Tend my sheep."
(John 21:16)

"Spend it (love) out. Don't testify how much you love Me, don't profess about the marvelous revelation you have had, but – "Feed My sheep." And Jesus has some extraordinarily funny sheep, some bedraggled, dirty sheep, some awkward butting sheep, some sheep that have gone astray!"– Oswald Chambers

The business of 'tending' someone else's sheep is a messy business indeed, primarily because you have so little say about the condition and kind of sheep the 'other' keeps. That will take some getting used to; especially if you intend to care for the kind of sheep Jesus keeps, those "extraordinarily funny" sheep who have found the Shepherd, or better yet, whom the Shepherd has found.

You will be tempted to think, "They must be like Jesus, after all, they are His sheep," but you couldn't be more wrong, and that is why 'tending His sheep' is so very difficult. More times than not, they are nothing like Him. His standard is so very low that almost any sheep, ok, any sheep, can gain access to His pens.

That will take some getting used to. His sheep, for all the instructions on how to be like Him, remain far too often, very much unlike Him. Thus, the idea of loving them out of 'natural' love toward them is just highly unlikely. Hence, the 'examination' by Him to make sure your love for Him is enough to sustain you, while you are 'spending it' toward sheep who are very often so preoccupied with 'life in general' and 'grazing' to even notice you are 'spending it' toward them. You cannot sustain your efforts at feeding, if your eyes are on the sheep; rather, you must see the 'Christ in them', the One whom you really love, if you are to continue the feeding that 'spends you' in the most exhausting ways.

Thus, you really understand His concern in determining if you really, really, really love Him. You simply will not be able to sustain tending this group of "extraordinarily funny sheep, some bedraggled sheep, dirty sheep, some awkward butting sheep, some sheep that have gone astray!" Then that startling moment of clarity, that comprehension that cannot be sidestepped, that horrific truth piercing the heart, arrives yet again. You, the one called to tend the sheep, are one of that motley flock.

Day 64

A LEISURE-HEARTED CALL?

"But I do not account my life of any value nor as precious to myself, if only I may finish my course and the ministry that I received from the Lord Jesus..."
(Acts 20:24)

"It is easier to serve God without a vision, easier to work for God without a call, because then you are not bothered by what God requires; commonsense is your guide, veneered over with Christian sentiment. You will be more prosperous and successful, more leisure-hearted, if you never realize the call of God."– Oswald Chambers

Those who have been 'called' by the King soon discover trekking after Him is not nearly so leisurely and 'spontaneous' as we would like to believe. Since few of the 'sheep' are genuinely 'called', but rather have simply 'wandered' into the pen, they will not understand the few who were 'called' and the strange way in which the 'called-out ones' describe their allegiance to the Serving King. Descriptors like 'slave' will seem odd to the crowd of those who have simply decided for 'this or that reason' to trek along with the Serving King.

Nor will the flock, those meandering along behind the Shepherd, understand the power the Shepherd seems to have over those who have 'heard' His call, more than that, have been 'claimed' by Him, following His every direction. The 'called-out ones' will indeed battle from time to time a sense of envy concerning the vast majority of the flock who have such a leisurely approach to life and obedience to the King. The 'called-out ones' may notice the 'other' sheep do indeed seem to have a "more prosperous and successful, more leisure-hearted" trek after the King.

But for the child of the Serving King who has been 'called out', a new realization begins to take root in the soil of the soul, an understanding changing everything, a new way of being and doing so profound it renders the 'life of leisure' moot, forgotten, no longer desired or sought after. That, of course, is the 'sign', the testimony, the proof, the verification you have indeed been 'called'. Your life, that journey of leisure and prosperity, no longer has any value at all. This 'valueless life' cannot be manufactured, willed into being, mandated into existence; to the contrary, it is simply the by-product of 'loving' the One Who has called you to "follow Me" and "feed My sheep." Have you heard this 'call' rendering the life of leisurely trekking after the Serving King moot?

Day 65
HAVE YOU SENSED JOY?

...if only I may finish my course and the ministry that I received from the Lord Jesus, to testify to the gospel of the grace of God. (Acts 20:24)

"Think of the satisfaction it will be to hear Jesus say– "Well done, good and faithful servant"; to know that you have done what He sent you to do. We have all to find our niche in life, and spiritually we find it when we receive our ministry from the Lord."– Oswald Chambers

For the child trekking after the King, joining the ranks of the 'few' who have not simply wandered into the sheep pen, instead 'called' directly by the Shepherd, every dimension of life is radically altered, redefined and given new meaning. Joy in life, that sense of purpose and accomplishment, will be reshaped and redescripted as well. No longer does the 'called' one assign joy, nor even sense joy, in the essence of the 'task' itself; instead, joy arrives in hearing the Shepherd say, "Well done, good and faithful servant." That is a significant shift.

That redescripting, more times than not, does not simply 'arrive'; rather, it must be cultivated and harvested by drawing ever so close to the 'Serving King', a closeness rendering the activity itself irrelevant and even insignificant. It is the 'presence' of the 'Serving King' that rewards, not the 'serving' itself, and the two ought never be confused. Only those who truly and profoundly 'love' the King can know the 'solitary reward' of being in the presence of the 'Serving King'. Richer yet, hearing His words of affirmation.

It is in that moment of 'joy', the child trekking after the 'Serving King' must pause and ask, "Is it the task that gives me joy, or is the presence of the 'Serving King' ushering in my joy?" This is a subtle but important distinction for those who hope to trek after the Serving King for a lifetime. For rest assured, not every task, not every serving, is inherently joyful; but the joy of serving alongside the 'Serving King' never fatigues. Those who trek next to the Serving King will never grow tired. Trek on...

Day 66

THE TRIVIAL TASK

But as servants of God we commend ourselves in every way: by great endurance, in afflictions, hardships, calamities...
(2 Corinthians 6:4)

"We flag when there is no vision, no uplift, but just the common round, the trivial task. The thing that tells in the long run for God and for men is the steady persevering work in the unseen, and the only way to keep the life uncrushed is to live looking to God. Ask God to keep the eyes of your spirit open to the Risen Christ, and it will be impossible for drudgery to damp you."– Oswald Chambers

For the child trekking after the 'Serving King' there is a temptation to affirm, "God would only 'call' me to serve in ways that bring joy and contentment," and that understanding is typically the case for those meandering after the King. But for those few 'called' by the 'Serving King' there is no such luxury of serving only in the 'pleasant fields'. To the contrary, it is indeed the "steady preserving work in the unseen, and the only way to keep the life uncrushed is to live looking to God."

The life of "endurance, in afflictions, hardships, calamities" and the like is rarely the life of the casual meanderer; rather, it is a journey reserved for the elite, the 'called-out ones', the 'ecclesia', who understand theirs is a life of 'sacrifice' in following the path of the 'Serving King'. However, the difficult part comes not in the 'sacrifice', nor even the particular 'task itself', but rather, the difficulty is sacrifice actualized in the realm of the 'unseen'. It is the 'unseenness' that 'crushes' the spirit of 'sacrificial service'.

It is in the solitude of serving in the 'fields of the unseen' that the child of the King must find the fellowship of the 'we' to which Paul alludes. It is the 'we', the other 'called-out ones' who know the fellowship of the 'we', a solitude of a special kind in the 'fields of the unseen', and the continued life of solitude accompanying those 'we' who serve and follow the "Shepherd Who calls." Indeed, it is a "long run for God," along the streets lined with no one, no spectators cheering, no cameras flashing, no coliseum filled with lions awaiting the spectacle of your 'life devoured' by the beasts as the throng roars with approval. No, it is the life of the mundanely 'unseen'.

Then you see Him, the only One that matters, the 'Significant Other' inside the 'we' of which Paul speaks, the One watching intently, the Christ, the One who proclaims, "Job well done, good and faithful servant." And the trivial and mundane vanish.

Day 67
TROUBLE OF A SPECIAL KIND

**No, in all these things we are more than conquerors
through Him who loved us.
(Romans 8:37)**

Paul is speaking of the things that might seem likely to separate or wedge in between the saint and the love of God; but the remarkable thing is that nothing can wedge in between the love of God and the saint. – Oswald Chambers

Moderns, those folks trekking after Jesus in the age of mobile phones and Ipads, often find it difficult to comprehend a life in which 'all these things' are experienced and even expected in the life of the child trekking after Jesus. But for those who are 'called', not simply meandering after Jesus, but 'called', it does not take long to understand Jesus never shies away from 'the road less travelled', the road of suffering; and more importantly, Jesus doesn't shy away from 'all these things' even when the 'children followers' are in tow, destined to experience 'all these things' simply because of their proximity to Jesus.

Thus, Paul announces it is the experience of 'all these things' that testifies to the reality the child of God is on the right path, the path Jesus Himself has trod. But it is important to understand that not every 'all these things' is the by-product of following Jesus. Many, if not most, of life's 'all these things' are the fruit of the sin and chaos that runs amuck in the modern era, and every other era for that matter. Hence, it is critical to keep Jesus within 'eyesight' at all times, especially in the midst of 'all these things' and to ask Him, "Is this 'all these things' the fruit of Your love for me, the consequence of my 'trekking after the King?'"

The answer will startle you yet again, for it is always the same, "Yes." The light slowly brightens in the mind's eye, slowly beginning to understand the redemptive love of Jesus is always at work, even in the midst of self-inflicted and consequential 'all these things'. It is the 'all these things' that molds, shapes, prods and caresses back onto the path He has trod. Of course, for those who have simply followed, who have never left the path, who have kept Jesus plainly in sight, it is the 'all these things' that bring about that final transformation into His likeness. And in that final moment of 'all these things', death itself, you realize fully and completely, "we are more than conquerors through Him Who loved us."

Day 68
THE TRAUMA OF STAGES

"I have been crucified with Christ..."
Galatians 2:20

No one is ever united with Jesus Christ until he is willing to relinquish not sin only, but his whole way of looking at things. To be born from above of the Spirit of God means that we must let go before we lay hold, and in the first stages it is the relinquishing of all pretense. – Oswald Chambers

Not long into the 'trek', the child of the Serving King begins to notice 'His ways' are not 'our ways', which, of course, is little cause for alarm, until that disheartening moment when the Serving King suggests you adopt 'His ways' as 'your ways'. That is problematic, generating another 'crisis', in a yet-to-come long series of 'crises' in which trekking after the King must be seriously reevaluated with each successive stage.

Now you will be tempted to think, with each successive crisis, you have settled the 'deal', given all there is to give, surrendered everything He has asked for in that particular moment; but it is becoming clearer and clearer to the child who stays in the trek, He is never done, every turn presenting a new 'stage', a new, closer look in which the Son peers even deeper into the core of your being.

Then, the child begins to understand as Jesus mines deeper and deeper into your being, the Son is no longer simply finding the 'bad', the 'ugly', the 'sin'; rather, the Son has found that which is 'good and pleasing'. Yet, even the 'good and pleasing' is not 'good and pleasing' enough. It, too, must go. It, too, the very best of your 'good and pleasing', must surrender to His way of 'being and doing', a way of 'being and doing' foreign to even your best 'good and pleasing'.

Then, it finally sinks in, "He intends to crucify me, all of me, not just the 'bad', the 'ugly' and the 'sin', but all of me, even the best of my 'good and pleasing.'" The trekker, without meaning to, pauses before the sight of the cross, instinctively knowing it will not be pleasant to walk this "Via Dolorosa", the way of grief, the road to the cross, the pathway to crucifixion. Dare you trek on after the Son? Follow Him to the cross? Trek on...

Day 69
DID YOU PAUSE?

**So Jesus said to the Twelve, 'Do you want to go away as well?"
(John 6:67)**

"They went back from walking with Jesus, not into sin, but they relapsed. Many today are spending and being spent in work for Jesus Christ, but they do not walk with Him..."– Oswald Chambers

For the 'meanderer', the one grazing leisurely after the Serving King, the question of 'going away' rarely comes. Theirs is a safe distance back from the Serving King, safely tucked away in the comfort of the flock, those who trek along in the safety of the mob. But those trekking closely after the Serving King, close enough to hear His voice, they will hear His every word and the sight of the 'Via Dolorosa' will cause pause even to the most faithful. Jesus, sensing the pause, simply asks, "Do you want to go away as well?"

It's a reasonable question given what is at stake, this 'crucified with Christ' (Galatians 2:20) looming ahead for the child trekking after the Serving King. You will need to give serious consideration to His probing examination. It will do no good to deflect the issue, for sooner or later, He will lead you down the 'Via Delorosa', it is the destination for every saint, every child trekking after the King, and all sheep must walk it at some point.

But the 'Via Dolorosa' cannot be navigated apart from Jesus. So be very careful not to allow Him to walk too far ahead of you. Being 'spent' apart from Jesus will not bring joy, or contentment, or a sense of accomplishment; no, it will produce only anxiety, as you attempt to 'turn away' from that which cannot be avoided. That is the great tragedy in life, turning away from that which cannot be avoided, and in doing so, missing the 'abundant life' awaiting those who have 'walked with Him', the full way, all the way, through the 'Via Dolorosa', to the life awaiting on the other side of 'crucifixion'. Resist the temptation to pause, to 'go away as well'; instead, carry on, stay close to Him. Abundant life waits for those who stay close, walking with Him, pushing through, enduring this 'crucifixion' that each one must know. Trek on...

Day 70

LIFESTYLE EVANGELISM?

**... preach the word; be ready in season and out of season.
(2 Timothy 4:2)**

"We are not turned into spiritual mediums, but into spiritual messengers; the message must be part of ourselves...There is a difference between giving a testimony and preaching."–
Oswald Chambers

Moderns have a love affair with 'lifestyle' evangelism, the idea that all a child trekking after the Serving King need do is trek and serve. Clearly, 'trekking and serving' are critical foundations for the next step, that uncomfortable moment when 'trekking and serving' have done all that 'trekking and serving' can do, that tilling of the soil, preparing soil to receive the 'Word', the 'seeds' with power to transform and give life. Therein lies the fundamental problem with 'trekking and serving' void of 'Word'. They are void, yes void, of transferrable power; for even attempts at mimicking will fall short, for the one who would mimic is missing the necessary 'power' for the activity longing to be mimicked.

Thus, Paul's challenge to those who have mastered the 'trek and serve' dimension of following after the Serving King; expand your skill set to include the most vital piece of the tools of evangelism: Preaching the Word. That is the next station of 'pause' for the child trekking after the Serving King. Lifestyle, especially in the 'land of the free', draws barely a glancing peek by those closeby, but 'preaching', speaking the 'why' of said 'lifestyle', is highly problematic for a politically correct culture of 'live as you will', but speak not! Preaching, or even 'speaking one's mind', is simply not allowed. The challenge to 'speak out', to 'preach', clearly places one's foot on the 'Via Dolorosa', the 'road less traveled, even by those trekking after the King.

Of course, you will be tempted to say, "Indeed, I will preach when the 'season' is right." But Paul will have none of that. There is no 'out of season' for the child trekking after the King. Yet, the children trek great distances, years on end in silence, living out 'lifestyle evangelism' with all the gusto of 'silent movie' stars on the 'big screen'. But then Paul asks, "When was the last time even you watched a 'silent movie'"? Trek on...

Day 71

THE PRACTICAL ISSUES

I was not disobedient to the heavenly vision...
(Acts 26:19)

"If we do not run our belief about God into practical issues, it is all up with the vision God has given. The only way to be obedient to the heavenly vision is to give our utmost for God's highest..."– Oswald Chambers

Trekking after the Serving King is lovely talk, right up to the moment when the 'theory' must find expression in 'practical issues', and it is that 'practicality' which is so illusive for the child trekking after the Serving King. 'Practicality' is simply the 'practice' of theory into day-to-day living, but it is illusive because the King does not provide step-by-step instructions for each individual journey; rather, that is the task of the one following the King. You must discover and actualize what living out 'practical issues' looks like in your unique journey after the King.

Be warned. It is the 'practical issues' that create the 'fuss' for the child trekking after the King, for it is only when you begin to act out the theory of the Kingdom in your everyday life that others will begin to notice your 'preaching' actually impacts your life and the life of those around you. It is the practical application that validates.

Preaching without 'acting out' is a harmless enough endeavor to those around you, as is the 'silent movie' of lifestyle evangelism, but when the two are combined into one life, a life that is real, verbal and relevant, then others will begin to feel the powerful conviction of the Holy Spirit in their lives. That is often not well received by those folks who coexist in your space.

Don't be surprised when those in the flock do not respond well to your 'practical approach' to life and ministry. They simply are not used to it. They have seen it modeled so rarely, striking them as odd, unusual, and even out of place. And that is the greatest proof of all that "if we do not run our belief about God into practical issues, it is all up with the vision God has given." Simply look around you and see the vast number of folks whose "utmost for God's highest" is simply embracing theory, while never finding those ever so critical 'practical issues'. Only those who can actually 'practice what they preach' will discover the meaning of "my utmost for His highest."

Day 72
COMMERCIAL INTEREST

**Peter began to say to Him, "See, we have left everything
and followed You."
(Mark 10:28)**

*"Our Lord replies, in effect, that abandonment is for Himself,
and not for what the disciples themselves will get from it.
Beware of an abandonment which has the commercial spirit
in it...If we only give up something to God because we want
more back, there is nothing of the Holy Spirit in our abandonment; it is miserable commercial self-interest."– Oswald
Chambers*

For the child trekking after the King, it is a horrible moment of self discovery, a sudden awareness that for all the magnificent change that has occurred while trekking after the Serving King, there really has been no change at all in the most fundamental arena of all. Those who have trekked before you called it the 'Second Crisis', that distasteful moment of insight coming only after many miles trekking alongside the King, when that flash of insight can no longer be ignored; instead, so simple and profound, so utterly 'on point', so piercing to the core of your being, you cannot help but 'pause' yet again at the sight of the 'cross' before you, empty and waiting for you to take that final step, to claim it as your own. Consecration awaits you yet again.

You will be tempted to join the chorus of Peter, "See, we have left everything and followed You!" But those words will not come, because this time there is no hiding from the truth, the self-realization that this journey has been the ultimate commercial enterprise, the grandest self-help scheme of all, the shrewdest of all investment plans, suddenly gone all wrong. Straightaway the opportunity to break free from 'self-interest' is replaced with a 'reckless abandonment of self' as your life is 'poured out' for Him, the Serving King.

Most surprising of all in this moment of self-discovery is an equally profound moment of understanding, the realization that giving your life for Him is okay, way okay; in fact, it is the very thing you most want to do. You are finally ready to leave behind that final aspect of your life: yourself. And, oh the joy of a journey so much lighter. Trek on in reckless abandonment.

Day 73
SO LOVED

"For God so loved the world, that He gave His only Son..."
(John 3:16)

In our abandonment we give ourselves over to God just as God gave Himself for us, without any calculation. The consequence of abandonment never enters into our outlook because our life is taken up with Him. – Oswald Chambers

Self-sacrifice, difficult as it may be, is a relatively small sacrifice for the child of the King, compared to the obedience of 'sacrificing others' for the sake of the Kingdom. The issue of sacrificing others would never arise if we could trek along after Jesus in 'isolation', just me and Jesus on the Jericho Road; but life in the Kingdom is never in isolation, 'others' are always impacted by our trekking. Thus, the sacrificial gift of the 'Son' functions not only as a powerful metaphor of how salvation was secured and paid for, but, in addition, sets an example of how life trekking after the King may have to function.

Indeed, this may be the ultimate, "Do you want to go away also" (John 6:67)? Mimicking the Son and His willingness to lay down His own life is one thing, but the call to consider 'laying down the life of another Isaac' is a far more troubling issue. Then, you remember the 'calling of Jesus' and His warning to those who would trek after Him, they, too, would have to 'lay down their own lives'. Jesus understood He would have to offer up the lives of those around Him, just as His Father had offered up the Son's life. Jesus mimicked the Father in offering up His followers, just as the Father was offering Him. A pattern begins to take shape.

The child trekking after the Serving King must be prepared for 'life sacrificed' by those who innocently follow along behind. This will never be easy. Be prepared to 'suffer' as those who have followed your lead in trekking after Jesus offer their lives sacrificially to the risen Lord. That is indeed the 'so loved' that you may be called to endure, a love so deep and profound it is willing to 'offer the other', the 'other' whom you have loved and cherished. Is there any greater turmoil than watching the sacrifice of the 'other offered up' for the Kingdom of God? "For God so loved the world, that He gave His only Son..."

Day 74

REDEMPTIVE REST

Do you not know that if you present yourselves to anyone as obedient slaves, you are slaves of the one whom you obey, either of sin, which leads to death, or of obedience, which leads to righteousness?
(Romans 6:16)

"Yield in childhood to selfishness, and you will find it the most enchaining tyranny on earth. There is no power in the human soul of itself to break the bondage of a disposition formed by yielding... There is no release in human power at all, but only in the Redemption."– Oswald Chambers

For those trekking after God, the trek itself will mandate the casting off of 'chains' that have enslaved since the days of childhood. Early on, those chains that can be thrown, are thrown, for the trek simply cannot be sustained without freeing oneself of the 'chains that so easily entangle'. But deeper into the journey, the 'chains' yet un-thrown become much heavier, more deeply entrenched in your being, and the discovery of self-limitation, the inability to cast them off, in spite of great effort to do so, begins to cripple the effort to stay on the heels of the Serving King. Then comes the discovery, 'release in human power' simply cannot be accomplished. These chains are too entrenched, too heavy, too 'enchaining' to be cast off in your own strength.

It is only through the liberation of 'redemption', the freeing power of the Christ, these remaining 'chains' can be cast off. That is the crowning moment of the journey thus far, the sudden realization the radical failure of 'self-effort' is not bad news; no, it is wonderful news, for now the power of the resurrected One comes to bear directly upon you and your weakness. It is He who sets free, Who redeems from those 'chains' too heavy for your 'self-effort'.

Thus, the glory of God begins to rain down upon you and the reign of the Spirit of the Living God begins to actualize in ways you have never dared to imagine. Suddenly, you understand you are being 'set free', redeemed in a magnificent way, transforming into the image of the One you have been trekking after. The glory of your lack of effort begins to manifest deeper and deeper into the core of your being. What a glorious rest as righteousness flows into your restfulness. And the obedience of the restful 'slave' becomes easier and easier.

Day 75

AFRAID?

Jesus was walking ahead of them. And they were amazed, and those who followed were afraid. And taking the twelve again... saying, "See, we are going up to Jerusalem, and the Son of Man will be delivered over... And they will mock Him and spit on Him, and flog Him and kill Him. And after three days He will rise."
(Mark 10:39-40)

"There is an aspect of Jesus that chills the heart of a disciple to the core and makes the whole spiritual life gasp for breath. This strange Being with His face set like a flint and His striding determination strikes terror into me. He is no longer Counsellor and Comrade, He is taken up with a point of view I know nothing about, and I am amazed at Him."– Oswald Chambers

You must never confuse the safety and security of the 'body of Christ' (the church) with the actual experience of trekking after the 'determined' Jesus. Jesus can never be 'tamed' and those who try to trek after Him are quick to learn that lesson. His single mindedness, regardless of 'cost', 'cost' to not just Himself, but equally applicable to those who trek after Him, is a cost that unnerves even the most committed trekker. His point of view is clearly not our normative point of view. His is a point of view loaded with a confidence concerning the assurance of resurrection and that knowledge changes everything.

Once death has been robbed of its power, the 'fear of death', it can no longer restrict or intimidate radical obedience to the call of God. That is what 'amazes' those who seek to imitate the Son. He has no 'fear of death', not concerning Himself, nor concerning those who will follow after Him. Death has no power. It has been rendered irrelevant. He clearly sees and knows a future that renders 'fear of death' moot.

And that is the moment in time every child trekking after the King longs for, that moment in which new life finds peace and contentment, even in the face of 'death', that moment when the follower can announce with certainty, "and they will mock me, and spit on me, and flog me, and kill me, and after death I will rise again." That is a profound moment of certainty rendering fear of both persecution and death powerless. In that moment, 'fear' is gone, and the 'power' and 'desire' to catch up to the Son Who walks ahead begins to flow. Trek on...

Day 76

THE DEATH OF SIN

For we must all appear before the judgment seat of Christ...
(2 Corinthians 5:10)

"One carnal judgment, and the end of it is hell in you. Drag it to the light at once and say– 'My God, I have been guilty there.' If you don't, hardness will come all through. The penalty of sin is confirmation in sin. It is not only God Who punishes for sin; sin confirms itself in the sinner and gives back full pay."– Oswald Chambers

The subtlety of 'sin' in the life of a child trekking after the King becomes harder and harder to see, to be cognizant of, to recognize for what it is, a cancer intent upon destroying and robbing life and vitality; especially for the child who has so radically improved their condition under the tutelage of the Holy Spirit. Nonetheless, 'sin' continues to be a constant threat to the health and vitality of the follower of Christ. You will be tempted to say, "I am forgiven of all my sin, secure in my relationship with the One Whom I am following." Indeed, no truer words have ever been thought.

But 'sin' is not a 'good loser', nor will it simply 'go quietly into the night'. No, 'sin' will continue to burrow its way into the depths of your being, determined to avoid the 'light of day' and the healing power of God's Word by finding the 'shadowlands' of your being. Thus, you must open your being to the probing presence of the Holy Spirit, guided by the 'light' of God's Word, to search and find the inner most hiding places of the 'sin' secretly lurking in the 'shadowlands'. Once found, you must judge 'sin' harshly, radically, completely and without mercy. But 'sin', hating the 'light', fighting for its very survival, will not simply 'come into the light'; instead, it will resist greatly, claiming to be 'light itself', even your friend. It will claim to be 'good' and 'helpful' in your journey to follow Christ, clothing itself in hideous, but lovely, self-righteousness.

Be very careful not to be persuaded by 'sin's' pleas of camaraderie. Know that you cannot see 'sin' for what it really is until you 'drag' it, kicking and screaming, into the 'light of day', for all the world to see. The power of the 'light' will kill it quickly and without mercy, for sooner or later, all 'sin' must face the 'judgment seat of Christ'. Judgment is never pleasant, now or later. But show no mercy. Sin must die.

Day 77
CROWD OF ONE

**So whether we are at home or away, we make it
our aim to please Him.
(2 Corinthians 5:9)**

*"It means holding one's self to the high ideal year in and
year out, not being ambitious to win souls or to establish
churches or to have revivals, but being ambitious only to be
'accepted of Him.' It is not lack of spiritual experience that
leads to failure, but lack of laboring to keep the ideal right.
Paul is like a musician who does not heed the approval of
the audience if he can catch the look of approval from his
Master."– Oswald Chambers*

The applause of the crowd, that group of folks who 'see' your trek after the King, is an incredibly addicting dimension within the human experience. Often, the trek starts in isolation, just you and the King, and only later, as you learn to 'be and do', both 'at home and away', does the crowd begin to notice you are on a trek, following an 'unseen leader', a leader who you seem to see with ease.

It is the 'scent' of the 'unseen leader' first catching the 'eye' of the crowd. It is pleasant enough at first, the waif of the 'leaders aroma' lingering upon your being, and the crowd smiles, graciously approving of your new 'being and doing', a pleasant 'newness' radiating from you. It feels good to hear the approval of the crowd. But as your trek after the King continues, the King's scent becomes increasingly noticeable as your 'being and doing' begins to morph into more pronounced ways of 'being and doing', clearly not your own. The 'invisible leader', whose scent was barely noticeable in those early days of your trek, begins to take shape before their eyes as your trek after the Serving King begins to produce an ever-increasing like-ness to the 'unseen leader'. Soon, the crowd begins to 'know' His presence, leading and creating this new way of 'being and doing' rendering a new you.

Then the crisis as you begin to notice the crowd, so approving of the 'puppy' you, that adorable first stage of morphing into the image of the 'unseen leader', is not nearly so approving of the 'post puppy' stage of trans-formation. The 'scent' of the 'unseen leader' is becoming a bit overbearing for the crowd. You sense they are not pleased. Now you must decide what your 'aim' really is, to please the crowd or do you make it "...our aim to please Him"? Are you content with a crowd of just Him?

Day 78
TO WHAT DEGREE

Since we have these promises, beloved, let us cleanse ourselves from every defilement of body and spirit, bringing holiness to completion in the fear of God.
(2 Corinthians 7:1)

"God educates us down to the scruple. When He begins to check, do not confer with flesh and blood, cleanse yourself at once... I have to cleanse myself from all filthiness of the flesh and spirit until both are in accord with the nature of God... I have the responsibility of keeping my spirit in agreement with His Spirit, and by degrees Jesus lifts me up to where He lived— in perfect consecration to His Father's will, paying no attention to any other thing." – Oswald Chambers

For those who stay on the trek, chasing after the ever moving Servant King, and that will not be everyone, for 'bringing holiness to completion' is a daunting task, the idea of 'degrees' is critical to understand. To 'bring holiness to completion' requires an understanding of precisely how "... by degrees Jesus lifts me up to where He lived." Fundamentally, it is as simple as one step at a time.

You will notice as you travel along that the Servant King does not 'transform' you in one comprehensive swoop. No, that would be too overwhelming, even for the most desiring child of the King. Instead, Jesus 'redeems' one piece of your being at a time, one degree at a time. Then He waits ever so patiently for "cleanse ourselves from every defilement of body and spirit" to unfold in our lives. Thus, we have stumbled upon the 'cog in the wheel' hindering maturity in Christ. It is this 'cleansing ourselves' in both 'body and spirit' as Jesus waits for the work to be done before moving onto the next 'degree'.

The process of 'cleanse ourselves' never finishes for "God educates us down to the scruple," that smallest amount of our being. It is never that God is done, but rather, God waits for our application of the 'redemption' that has arrived in us to work 'its' way out into the very 'being and doing' of the child who must 'cleanse every defilement of body and spirit' before the next 'degree' of redemption will be brought to bear on your 'body and spirit'. Then comes the question, "To what degree of my 180° turn am I presently at?" Know this, you will not continue to 'turn' until you have 'cleansed yourself from every defilement of body and spirit...'" Trek on...

Day 79
EXCHANGING THE KITH

**"By faith Abraham obeyed when he was called to go out to a place that he was to receive as an inheritance. And he went out, not knowing where he was going.
(Hebrews 11:8)**

"In the Old Testament, personal relationship with God showed itself in separation, and this is symbolized in the life of Abraham by his separation from his country and from his kith and kin. Today the separation is more of a mental and moral separation from the way that those who are dearest to us look at things, that is, if they have not a personal relationship with God."– Oswald Chambers

The early days of the trek after the Serving King meander in familiar lands, close to your 'kith', your clan and all that is familiar; but that typically will not last. Indeed, the loss of familiar surroundings, the mountains, plains and seas you have always known is merely setting the stage for the real work that has to be done, the exchange of one value system for another. A complete overhaul more comprehensive than you can understand or embrace while reclining in the old 'kith', may be required.

It is the 'exchange' of one 'kith' for another 'kith' that proves difficult, for the trekker soon learns that "His ways are not our ways" (Isaiah 55:8-9). This 'mental and moral' separation is a difficult trek indeed. Early on, you will attempt to simply merge the 'kith' of God into your own historical 'kith', searching for points of commonality, delighting when you discover accidental points of congruency, resting in those moments of relief as you anticipate God's 'kith' to be similar to your historic 'kith'. But you will soon discover, you could not be more wrong. It is an inevitable. Eventually, you simply have to leave the old 'kith' behind as the new way of 'being and doing' emerges. It is simply God's way.

So, God begins the process for Abraham by simply telling him to leave the physical 'kith' behind, completely behind, gathering up his immediate family to go, "not knowing where he was going." As difficult as the trek has been, the child trekking after the Serving King suddenly realizes, "He's taking me away from home, the places and the people, the values and the ways of 'being and doing' that have always been so comfortable, so easy." Then you will 'pause' again, wondering if life without the old 'kith' can be 'abundant'? Is it safe to travel with this 'Serving King' into unknown ways of 'being and doing'? Walk on "to a place that he was going to receive as an inheritance." Trek on...

Day 80
RIGHTLY RELATED

**The Lord said, "Shall I hide from Abraham what I am about to do..."
(Genesis 18:17-18)**

"When you are rightly related to God, it is a life of freedom and liberty and delight, you are God's will, and all your commonsense decisions are His will for you unless He checks. You decide things in perfect, delightful friendship with God, knowing that if your decisions are wrong He will always check; when He checks, stop at once."– Oswald Chambers

The reality that 'God's ways are not our ways' (Isaiah 55:8-9) brings a moment of awkwardness between God and the child trekking after the Serving King. It causes God to 'pause' and to ask, "Shall I hide from the child what I am about to do?" God's concern for our ability to 'handle' 'His ways' reminds the child trekking after the King there is still a long way to go in coming to understand 'God's ways'; more importantly, accepting and affirming 'God's ways'. But God is careful with us, gentle even, considering 'when and how' His ways should be introduced into the life of each Christ follower.

Therein lies a clue toward understanding when 'God's ways' have indeed become your ways. The condition of 'rightly related', immersed in the ways of God, will produce a 'common sense' relationship with God in which your new way of 'being and doing' gracefully reflects God's way of 'being and doing'. As 'His way' becomes 'your way', that common sense way of 'being and doing' will operate increasingly, rendering the need for 'new revelation' to decrease with each passing day. Common sense begins to reflect God's way of 'being and doing', becoming 'second nature'.

However, from time to time, it would be beneficial to pause and ask, "God, am I on the same page You are, like-minded, moving in sync with You, on the same common sense path? Or am I simply at that place in my journey that You don't think I can handle Your 'ways'? Are You still having to protect me from 'ways' that I will not understand nor be able to accept and affirm?" Never assume there is not more of 'God's way' yet to come than what you have received to date. You might be surprised at how much God is still pondering, "Shall I hide from Abraham what I am about to do?" Trek on that you might see more.

Day 81
CRUCIFIED?

**I have been crucified with Christ.
(Galatians 2:20)**

"'… nevertheless I live …' The individuality remains, but the mainspring, the ruling disposition, is radically altered. The same human body remains, but the old satanic right to myself is destroyed."– Oswald Chambers

The serpent, Satan, has long been committed to a basic strategy when dealing with those in a profound relationship with God (Genesis 3), and it succeeds because there is something inherent in our being connecting with the serpent's suggestion of God's intent to 'restrict and limit' the human condition. The 'Fall' damages even further that fundamental thread running through each and every child trekking after the Serving King, a thread proclaiming some concept of fundamental entitlements, foremost of which is the right to 'be all you can be'. It is that 'be all you can be thread' which must be dealt with in the most drastic way possible.

Therein lies the 'fundamental' problem: You cannot perform 'suicidal crucifixion' try as you may. Only God, through the power of the Holy Spirit, can 'crucify with Christ'. You can desire 'crucified with Christ' so comprehensively that you offer your body 'as a living sacrifice' (Roman 12:1). But do not be surprised when that 'thread', corrupted as it is, weaves itself around even your sincerest attempts to offer your life and body as a 'living sacrifice' unto God.

The best you can hope for, as you wait for 'crucifixion', is to manage the 'right to be all you can be'. That will take a great deal of effort, for this 'thread' of self-interest and self-enhancement so easily entangles, so easily wraps itself in and around even the best of your intentions. But manage it you must until God decides the time has come, you are ready for "crucified with Christ."

When it occurs, like Paul, you will know when 'the mainspring, the ruling disposition, is radically altered', as your inner being experiences a profound correction rendering 'self-interest' moot. You will then join Paul in making a simple and quiet announcement, "I have been crucified with Christ." The internal struggle is over. And you quietly return to the trek.

Day 82
OPENING THE SCRIPTURES

They said to each other, "Did not our hearts burn within us while He talked to us on the road, while He opened to us the Scriptures?" (Luke 24:35)

"It is the dull, bald, dreary, commonplace day, with commonplace duties and people, that kills the burning heart unless we have learned the secret of abiding in Jesus."–Oswald Chambers

It will not take long for the child trekking after the Serving King to fatigue of the 'commonness' of serving, and that is to be expected, for there is no 'inherent' joy in the mundane task of service. Nor will those being served stand and cheer you onward, nor will the crowd of followers take time to applaud your mundane service. But relief can be found, relief that soothes and encourages the child engaged in mundane service. The first is to never lose sight of Jesus, engaging only in what Jesus has called for. Never confuse 'service' in general with 'serving alongside the King'. There is a profound difference. The latter will be rewarding, the former simply 'kills the burning heart' as the tyranny of the mundane, apart from Jesus, suffocates the 'burning heart'.

The second is the 'mystery' of intimate fellowship with Christ through His written Word, and, sadly, it occurs for far too few of those trekking at a safe distance behind Jesus. It is 'opening of the Word' that occurs for those who 'talk' with Jesus while on the trek. Scholars have longed for it, this 'revelation', this seeing beyond the mere words on a page, this depth of insight into the mystery of God's Word, a mystery sages have longed for, but given only to those who 'walk along the road' with Jesus.

This 'walking revelation' is a special kind of 'mystery' illuminating the 'mundane service' of the 'crucified life'. It will not inspire the scholar, nor the sage, nor those unengaged in 'mundane service'; no, this is a special kind of 'mystery' providing insight into the 'how and why' of the mundane, a 'crucified life' spent in service alongside the King. That is the 'secret of abiding in Jesus'. It is the 'burning heart' hearing the voice of Jesus, those precious 'coals' for the fire of the heart in the mundane commonplace of life. When He speaks, listen ever so carefully, for without those 'coals of insight' for the heart, it is destined to 'burn out', ever so quietly, as the soul sinks deeper and deeper into the mundane commonplace of life.

Day 83
AND THE BATTLE CONTINUES

**For you are still of the flesh. For while there is jealousy and strife among you, are you not of the flesh and behaving only in a human way?
(1 Corinthians 3:3)**

"No natural man knows anything about carnality. The flesh lusting against the Spirit that came in at regeneration, and the Spirit lusting against the flesh, produces carnality."– Oswald Chambers

'Carnality', 'behaving only in a human way', is a frustrating reality for the child trekking after the Serving King, a King Who demands His followers walk in a particular way, a way resembling His walk. That 'way of walking', of being and doing, is not 'natural' to the newcomer, nor even the longtime trekker; instead, it requires a constant vigil against the 'flesh', that carnal way of being and doing that comes so 'naturally', so easily, after so many years of practice.

It is the 'longtime trekker' who struggles, fatigues of the relentless battle deep within the 'flesh', wondering when the 'walking in the Spirit' will be as 'natural' as the seemingly endless 'walking in the flesh', continuing year after year, as the trek after Jesus continues. However, the skirmishes change as maturity becomes a reality for the child of God. The early battles of 'jealously and strife' begin to fade into the distance as the Spirit of the Living God moves deeper and deeper into your being, looking for well camouflaged pockets of resistance having draped themselves in the platitudes of righteousness and the ways of God, but secretly still operate in the 'realm of the flesh', the old ways of being and doing.

It is only deep into the journey that the child trekking after the King finally begins to understand 'behaving only in a human way' cannot continue in the 'Spirit-filled life', the Spirit simply will not allow it. Instead, the 'Spirit lusting against the flesh' probes deeper and deeper, declaring war against every residual 'flesh' way of being and doing. But the 'flesh' will call to its old ally, its oldest friend, the one who has 'fed it' and sustained it through every previous battle, the one counted on so dependably in so many previous skirmishes: you. Then you will have to decide. Will you war with the Spirit against the 'flesh', or will you once again rescue an old reliable partner? Be prepared for the pleas of distress from your old ally. You will literally feel its pain as the Spirit vanquishes it. Be strong and walk on in the Spirit.

Day 84

THE HUMILITY OF DECREASE

He must increase, but I must decrease...
(John 3:30)

"If you become a necessity to a soul, you are out of God's order."– Oswald Chambers

At some point, deep into the journey, entrenched in the life of service, that 'soul' which you have dreamed and longed for, the one who finally embraces what you are offering, appears before you, walks with you, trekking behind the Serving King. Oh, how you have longed for a companion, someone to walk with, to talk to, who values this trek after Jesus you have been on, month after month, year after year. What joy to finally find that kindred spirit to journey with.

You must, however, be very alert in this journey with the 'other' that Jesus remains the primary relationship, for both you and the 'other', and that will not be easy. Instead, you will be tempted to allow the 'others', spouse, family, friend, etc., to become your primary relationship, and the trek after Jesus, the Serving King, becomes unintentionally secondary. This 'falling behind' Jesus in the journey will not have intentionality, nor will it happen quickly, but it will happen, ever so slowly, to those losing focus on the 'ever-moving Servant King'.

The symptoms of this transition away from the 'coattails' of Jesus are not difficult to spot. You will begin to notice worship must always be 'communal', rather than in isolation. Prayer moves from that 'solitary' experience in the 'closet' toward a 'social' event with 'others'. Study of the Word, that 'revelatory' encounter with the Risen Christ, can only be experienced in the company of the many rather than an encounter with your personal Tutor. Alone time with Jesus becomes rarer and rarer.

Then the realization strikes you, confronts you, convicts you. The 'other' you have journeyed with has not learned to walk alone, without you; treading instead alongside the Serving King, forgetting who 'you' are for the moment, leaving you isolated once again in this trek after Jesus. And a tinge of fear strikes you, "What if they don't come back to walk with me? What if they carry on only with the Serving King?" Then you realize that difficult lesson, "He must increase, but I must decrease." Walk on with Him. He is all you need.

Day 85
THE DESTINATION OF DECREASE

**The friend of the bridegroom, who stands and hears him, rejoices greatly at the bridegroom's voice...
(John 3:29)**

"Goodness and purity ought never to attract attention to themselves, they ought simply to be magnets to draw to Jesus Christ. If my holiness is not drawing towards Him, it is not holiness of the right order, but an influence that will awaken inordinate affection and lead souls away into side-eddies."– Oswald Chambers

It is a difficult thing to think 'less' of oneself when praise, praise accurate and true, is thrown at your feet, by an ever-increasing number of folks who 'see' the genuine change taking place in your life. Trekking closely with Jesus by definition will bring change throughout a lifetime, thus the danger of 'side-eddies' for those watching you will be a constant threat. In those moments, you will take great effort to deflect the praise to Jesus, but to no avail, it is too late, the credit has already been launched and recorded in the mind of the one sticking the praise to your 'wall'.

Therein lies one of the great challenges of the trek after Jesus: How to insure others are drawn to Jesus and not you. The Apostles provide great clues to avoiding these 'side-eddies'. Consider the Apostle John for a few moments. Recite everything you know about the Apostle John. Notice how little there is to recite? But you can tell his story of Jesus, the Word becoming flesh (John 1) and the many tales concerning the Serving King, who gave His life as a ransom for the many. That is the secret to the 'destination of decrease'. Talk about Jesus. Incessantly talk about the Bridegroom.

You will soon discover that those around you know very little of your story. But they know volumes of His story. Live authentically, openly, and those trekking with you will know there is still much yet to be done in you. For as the saying goes, "Be patient with me, God isn't finished with me yet." Then talk about Jesus as you walk on.

Day 86

THE UNWANTED COMPANION

**Blessed are the pure in heart, for they shall see God.
(Matthew 5:8)**

"Purity is not innocence, it is much more. Purity is the outcome of sustained spiritual sympathy with God. We have to grow in purity. The life with God may be right and the inner purity remain unsullied, and yet every now and again the bloom on the outside may be sullied."– Oswald Chambers

Those who seriously trek after 'purity' soon come to realize it is not as simple as 'purity of heart' and mind, precisely because the 'pure heart' must find ways to express itself in a sullied existence. You will be tempted to think the 'sullied existence' is always 'out there', those sullied conditions, sullied 'others' with whom you must interact, and nothing can be done about it. Indeed, the world in which the trek must take place is a 'sullied place' filled with 'sullied others'. But it is not as simple as that.

Paul, long into his trek with the Serving King, discovered a painful reality often haunting any child seriously trekking after purity, "So now it is no longer I who do it, but sin that dwells within me. For I know that nothing good dwells in me, that is, in my flesh. For I have the desire to do what is right, but not the ability to carry it out" (Romans 7:17). His statement is not a declaration of 'everyday' life trekking after the King, filled with countless successes in the imitation of the King; no, it is the ultimate reality for any child who desperately wants not just countless victories, but 'purity' of 'being and doing'. It is the standard of 'purity', of 'perfection', of 'Christlikeness', driving the child of the King to utter desperation and exasperation, "Wretched man that I am! Who will save me from this body of death?" (Romans 7:24)

Tragically, for those who seek 'purity of being and doing', the reality of the unwanted companion, "making me captive to the law of sin that dwells in my members" (Romans 7:23), lives on in the 'flesh' (body). Purity of 'being and doing' will simply not happen in this immediate trek after Jesus. That is the reality of a glory yet to come. Then the blessed reminder, "Blessed are the pure in heart, for they shall see God." So the 'war' begins, continues, as the 'unwanted companion' must be hunted down, dragged into the 'city square' and destroyed, piece by piece, until the illusion of 'purity of being and doing' begins to appear.

Day 87

THE DANGER OF CONTENTMENT

**"Come up here, and I will show you what must take place after this."
(Revelation 4:1)**

"An elevated mood can only come out of an elevated habit of personal character. If in the externals of your life you live up to the highest you know, God will continually say– 'Friend, go up higher.'"– Oswald Chambers

There comes a point for the child trekking after the Serving King, when the reality of 'falling away' becomes diminutive from the perspective of the 'one' who would love to see a 'falling away', the 'evil one'. Thus, a change of tactic is required to diminish the effectiveness of those trekking closely with Jesus, the creation of a 'state of contentment', arriving at that place where the child is 'content' in who and what they have become. And to be fair, it is startling how 'low' some will set that 'bar' of personal trans-formation. Contentment comes far too easily for many.

The One who leads will have none of that. His call is ever upward, ever 'your utmost, for His highest'. Thus, He will say, "as long as today is called today, come up here, and I will show you what must take place after this." But you will want to savor the 'this' for days on end, for the 'this' was not easy; to the contrary, the 'this' required a great deal of effort leaving a residue of fatigue, a crippling fatigue at times. That is why He is ever so careful to keep the 'come up here' within reach of a fatigued child. It is literally a 'one step at a time' process.

Nonetheless, crippling as the 'fatigue' can be, it is the sense of 'con-tentment' ultimately undermining any further effort to offer 'your utmost for His highest'. Contentment will whisper in your ear, "Look how far you have come! Look how others have lagged behind in the trek after the Serving King. You deserve a reprieve from this ever-present challenge to 'come up here'. Relax and celebrate in worship of the King! Praise Him for what He has done!" 'Contentment', bathed in fatigue, offers a glorious moment of rest cozied up in the presence of 'praise and wor-ship', a moment that will only be for the 'moment', a 'pause' that expands in duration with every passing day. This 'moment' suddenly becomes a 'state of being', the 'state of 'contentment', a dangerous foe to the child who previously knew no such condition. Shake off this 'state of content-ment', hear His voice, "Come up here, and I will show you what must take place after this." There is trekking forward yet to be done.

Day 88
COME UP HERE AGAIN

Then after this He said to the disciples, "Let us go to Judea again." The disciples said to Him, "Rabbi, the Jews were just now seeking to stone You, and are You going there again?" (John 11:7-8)

"Are you loyal to Jesus or loyal to your notion of Him? Are you loyal to what He says, or are you trying to compromise with conceptions which never came from Him? 'Whatsoever He saith unto you, do it.'"– Oswald Chambers

Part of the 'come up here' process is the revisiting of previous 'failures' in the life of a child trekking after the Serving King. That will be difficult. You will want to say, "That didn't go well last time I followed You there. Things got ugly. Folks were looking to stone You and me, to abuse me, take advantage of me." Worse yet, you will be tempted to 'reason' with Jesus, to remind Him of just how bad things really got for both of you and why the attempt to 'come up here' should not be made again. It is not easy to 'go to Judea again'.

The process of transformation, this becoming like Him, will include many visits to places and people that 'did not go well', the 'Judeas' of your life. That, of course, is what makes the trek so difficult for those who are seeking 'Christlikeness'. Failure is simply not an option. So, He will call you again and again to 'come up here and let us do this again', this revisiting of Judea.

Nonetheless, never confuse 'come up here again' with your own misguided initiative. There is a profound difference in 'climbing to the top of the mountain' with the Serving King as He calls and simply determining to 'climb to the top of the mountain' out of your own determination. The latter, well intentioned as it may be, is doomed to failure and chaos. You simply are not ready for that steep a climb, else He would have called, "Come up here" already. You will discover you are not well equipped for the climb, nor for determining which climbs to attempt, only He knows the 'where and when' of your next Judea. Resist the temptation to say, "Let us go back to Judea again," even when you are sure you can do it this time. Instead, wait patiently for Him to initiate this difficult trek back to Judea. His timing is everything when 'going back to Judea'. Trek after Him and your 'Judeas' will all reappear soon enough. Walk on...

Day 89
THE WORKERS TEMPTATION

"You also must be ready, for the Son of Man is coming at an hour you do not expect."
(Luke 12:40)

"The great need for the Christian worker is to be ready to face Jesus Christ at any and every turn...If we are going to be ready for Jesus Christ, we have to stop being religious (that is, using religion as a higher kind of culture) and be spiritually real."– Oswald Chambers

No worker trekking after the Serving King has aspirations of being a 'maintenance worker' dedicated to the care and prolongation of the religious culture, frequently called the 'church'. The 'church', never to be confused with 'The Church', the Body of Christ, has a way of seducing the 'worker' set on the path of trekking after Jesus. The church is crafty in its seduction, clothing itself in the cares and concerns of the Serving King; nonetheless, more frequently concerned about its own continued viability than the actual 'business' of helping the children of the King to trek closely in His footsteps. Or, more importantly, helping lost children to find their way to the King. But the seduction is deeper yet for that rare worker, the one who finds sustenance for life, food and shelter, from the tit of the 'church'. That worker, 'seduced' by the life-giving sustenance from the 'church', will find the temptation to be 'religious, "that is, using religion as a higher kind of culture", overwhelming at times; sometimes so overwhelming the call of Jesus to 'trek on' will be lost in the lust for 'sustenance', those life-giving resources the 'church' doles out to obedient maintenance workers who resist the beckoning of Jesus upon their lives, and 'stay put', absorbed and lost in the work of the 'church'.

Thus, it becomes critical for the 'worker' to pause in their 'work' of religion, and to look around to see if Jesus is still anywhere near? For if He is gone, then the 'worker' has succumbed to simply 'being religious', has become a 'maintenance worker' prolonging and caring for the 'church', while the authentic Church, the Body of Christ, has continued along the trek, never losing sight of the Serving King, staying close by His side. Then you will remember, "You must also be ready, for the Son of Man is coming at an hour you do not expect." Then the meaning of 'be ready' becomes ever so clear. Never lose sight of the 'Serving King' less you fall into the trap of 'being religious', seduced by the 'religious culture': the 'church'. The 'Church' can always be found only at the side of Jesus.

Day 90
BEWARE THE SNARE

**He saw that there was no man, and wondered that
there was no one to intercede...
(Isaiah 59:16)**

*"'But there is no one interceding properly'– then be that one
yourself, be the one who worships God and who lives in holy
relationship to him. Get into the real work of intercession,
and remember it is a work, a work that taxes every power;
but a work which has no snare. Preaching the gospel has a
snare; intercessory prayer has none."– Oswald Chambers*

For some 'workers', those children trekking relentlessly after the
Serving King, the 'hard work' of intercessory prayer, that 'closet-dwelling'
role of isolation with the Serving King, will never be accomplished. Other
versions of 'prayer', especially those public displays of prayer in praise
and worship in the community of fellow trekkers, will abound, but the 'hard
work', "a work that taxes every power", will remain undone, neglected by
a generation of workers who know only the 'work of movement', rather
than the 'hard work' of 'isolated intercessory prayer', stillness before
God producing utter exhaustion.

The 'work of the closet', done in isolation, can never be shared with
another; hence, it is too often relegated to the work of tomorrow. Today's
work will be in the company of the 'others'. Like all work done in the
'Spirit', 'intercessory prayer' is the most productive kind of work, though
typically not nearly as fast as one would like it to be; and because it is
done in isolation, there will be no 'snares' for the worker.

It is those 'snares', the rewards of praise and acknowledgement,
seducing the worker away from intercessory prayer. Work that can be
seen is work for which credit can be given. However, the work of isolation
in prayer, by its very nature, must be unseen, unknown, even to the one
who has reaped the benefit of your hard work. And they will wonder, "Who
has done this for me?" But the 'isolated worker' is nowhere to be seen,
hidden in the 'prayer closest', exhausted from "a work that taxes every
power." Beware the snare that awaits just outside the 'closet', the nagging need to humbly and publicly give credit to the "God who answered
your prayer." For in that moment of 'praise to God', intercessory prayer
has ended and caught in the snare you are. In unknown isolation you
must stay, if you are to 'beware the snare'.

Day 91
THE DARK SIDE OF SEEING

If anyone sees his brother committing a sin not leading to death, he shall ask, and God will give him life – to those who commit sins that do not lead to death.
(1 John 5:16)

"One of the subtlest burdens God ever puts on us as saints is this burden of discernment concerning other souls. He reveals things in order that we may take the burden of these souls before Him..." – Oswald Chambers

For the child trekking close with the Serving King, there will be some dimensions of 'Spiritual' insights the trekker would rather do without. Case in point, 'insight' into the soul of another fellow trekker. Not every insight into the soul of another will be pleasant. At times, you will be tempted to look away, rather than be engaged in the hard work of 'redemptive intercessory prayer'. Or, even more trying, you will first be tempted to approach this fellow trekker in an attempt to help give insight into the error of their way, but neither looking away or approaching is the first step. The first step is always the hard work of intercessory prayer.

It is in the hard work of intercessory prayer that the redemptive power of God is unleashed without the awkwardness of confrontation concerning another's weakness, or the even more awkward, 'looking the other way'. Instead, by intercessory prayer, the redemption that need occur is unleashed as God responds to the hard work of intercession on the part of the intercessor. Again, the work must be done in the 'closet' and never brought into the light of day, even if the transgressor should say, "God has helped me with this." You must resist the temptation to create that awkwardness of 'unknown insight' by suggesting, "Yes, I have been praying for you in that area." Instead, the 'hard work' must remain in the 'closet'.

Then comes the hardest part. You must throw what has been seen into the 'sea of forgetfulness', just as God does. It is in that moment of forgetfulness that the image of a fellow trekker is left unscathed, bathed in the redemption of God, for "God will give him life," no, has given him life, in this case. It is the redeemed life that you must see again. It is only when you 'see as God sees' that the "subtlest burden" is laid aside, forgotten, drowned in that 'sea of forgetfulness'. Never continue to carry unnecessary 'subtle burdens'.

99

Day 92

DO THE HARD WORK

**Christ Jesus is the One Who died—more than that,
Who was raised—Who is at the right hand of God,
Who indeed is interceding for us.
(Romans 8:34)**

"...get into such living relationship with God that our relationship to others may be maintained on the line of intercession whereby God works His marvels. Beware of outstripping God by your very longing to do His will. We run ahead of Him in a thousand and one activities, consequently we get so burdened with persons and with difficulties that we do not worship God, we do not intercede."– Oswald Chambers

The temptation to 'do', rather than allow God to 'do', is problematic, in an ongoing way, for the child trekking after the 'Serving King'. The assumption far too many trekkers make is simply, "If He is serving, then I should be serving," 'doing for' and toward others. This is especially true in those areas of life in which you can 'do', as compared to those other areas in life that are simply beyond your 'doing'. Intercession in those areas beyond your 'doing' will come naturally, almost easily, for 'it', the 'doing', is simply beyond your capability and resources.

The temptation will come when you have the resources and ability to 'do', to serve, mimicking the pattern of the 'Serving King'; rather than doing the 'hard work' first: interceding. In doing the easy work, the 'doing', without first 'interceding', you will indeed often, "run ahead of Him in a thousand and one activities." And ahead of Him is no better than 'behind Him'. Either way, you are by yourself.

However, for the child who learns to do the 'hard work' first, this 'interceding', just as He and the Holy Spirit first interceded (Romans 8:24), a marvelous pattern will begin to unfold. First, "our relationship to others may be maintained on the line of intercession whereby God works His marvels." Note, 'God works' rather than 'you work'. But be of good cheer, those desperately longing 'to do', because when you have finally learned to do the 'hard work' of intercession, you may indeed discover God has a 'do' for you 'to do'. Thus comes the marvelous moment in which you are a vital part of "whereby God works His marvels." There is yet plenty 'to do' while trekking after the Serving King, but first, slow down and do the 'hard work'.

Day 93
THE SEEING BLIND

...the Lord Jesus Who appeared to you on the road by which you came has sent me so that you may regain your sight.
(Acts 9:17)

"When Paul received his sight he received spiritually an insight into the Person of Jesus Christ."– Oswald Chambers

Saul, who would soon become Paul, had been blind for a very long time; though sadly, he was completely unaware, seeing the same old patterns repeatedly. That is not uncommon for those who have lived in the shadow of the 'religious' for a very long time. His blindness, the inability to see anything 'new', in spite of 'eyes wide open', incapacitated him for work in the Kingdom of God. This blindness, the by-product of hardening of the spiritual mind, is not uncommon in the world of the church, or any community of believers; rather, it is tragically common, rendering many 'useless' for Kingdom building.

Nonetheless, this 'eyes wide open' blindness is dangerous for those so inflicted, both to themselves, and to those whom they will stumble into, all in the name of 'righteousness'. For some, the blind meandering will simply become a way of life, and those so afflicted will learn the 'patterns' of living together in the community of the religious, insisting that 'change' never be implemented, rendering it impossible for the 'blind' to function, stumbling around in a world that has been rearranged by someone whose sight has been restored.

For those determined to trek after the ever Serving King, 'eyes wide open' blindness will never do. They will fatigue of seeing the same thing, repeatedly, walking and stumbling along the same paths, day after day, conversing in the same way, with the same folks, hour after hour. Then that horrific moment when 'awareness' of the repetition, the endlessly repeating pattern, becomes so clearly seen, you realize you are 'blind', looking at the same picture without end.

Then, you hear this one whom God "has sent so that you may regain your sight." In that moment comes a single ray of 'insight', a newness of understanding, a different road appears before you, and you must decide, "Shall I stay in the safety of the old patterns, or follow the 'newness' that God has before me?"

Day 94

HIDDEN FROM VIEW

"Would that you, even you, had known on this day the things that make for peace! But now they are hidden from your eyes." (Luke 19:42)

"These words imply culpable responsibility; God holds us responsible for what we do not see. 'Now they are hid from thine eyes'– because the disposition has never been yielded."– Oswald Chambers

Never assume regaining your sight means you can see 'everything' that ought to be seen. To the contrary, there are a good many things 'hidden' from your sight simply because you have not removed those 'things' which hide them, things like "the disposition that has never been yielded." Tragically, Jesus warned 'peace' cannot be found until you are able to 'see' what it is 'God' is doing in the midst of the seeming chaos. "...even you, had known on this day the things that make for peace."

Therein lies one of the greatest 'gifts' of all, the ability to see the 'hand of God' weaving the tapestry of your life. Too often, the 'hand of God' is hidden from view by "the disposition (that) has never been yielded." You will be tempted in those moments to believe, "If I cannot see the Serving King's hand, then God cannot be at work, weaving as only God can." It is in that moment the opportunity arises to remove a serious barrier to seeing God at work, the barrier of 'doubt'.

It was 'doubt', in spite of all the visible indicators, keeping the disciples from receiving the good news of the resurrection. Ever-present 'doubt' kept them from seeing what was right before their eyes, the marvelous movement of God, the resurrected Christ. Doubt is an immense barrier in the life of a child trekking after the King.

Thus, to see 'all' that can be seen, the child trekking after the Serving King must learn to gain mastery over 'doubt', for it is a constant companion, hindering the ability to 'see' all that can be seen. The key to seeing the redemptive ever-present hand of God in the midst of the chaos is the assurance 'the hand' is there. Look deeper. See what you know must be there, the "hand of God' weaving the circumstances of your life into a fabric bringing 'peace' for those who 'see the weaver's hand'. Look deeper as you trek further along the tapestry God has woven just for you.

Day 95
WORKING OUT THE DETAILS

"Behold, the hour is coming, indeed it has come, when you will be
scattered, each to his own home, and will leave Me alone."
(John 16:32)

"After we have been perfectly related to God in sanctification, our faith has to be worked out in actualities."–Oswald
Chambers

With the gift of 'seeing' comes revelation, a wealth of insight into the
ways of God, customized for the unique journey every child trekking after
the 'Serving King' must travel. However, this 'seeing', insight into the
ways of God, comes initially in a 'generic' format, general principles that
must find expression in the 'actualities' of your unique journey and therein
begins the actual 'consequences' of trekking after the 'Serving King'.

Consequences, those repercussions from the 'actualities' of putting
revelation, the fruit of 'seeing', into practice, can often create the temptation to 'scatter', to distance yourself from Jesus. The scattering, returning
to 'your own home', is simply the by product of 'consequences' arising
when "our faith has to be worked out in actualities." It is not the 'trekking
with Jesus' causing you to 'scatter'; to the contrary, the child trekking
after the King and the King have become quite fond of each other. No,
it is simply the 'consequences' of turning the 'principles' of the King into
'actualities, laden with 'consequences', many of which are not pleasant
or pleasing.

As the saying goes, "You can never go back home" and that is never
more true than attempting to return 'home', the 'old ways of being and
doing', following your extensive trek with the Serving King. Home is no
longer the place you left long ago to trek after the King. You have new
eyes, a new way of 'being and doing', new values, etc. It is upon the return
'home', a trip that will not be a pleasant homecoming, that the child trekking after the King will suddenly understand a startling revelation: "I am a
new creation in Christ and the home I left is no longer comfortable for me."

Then a wonderful 'revelation', a moment of 'seeing', flashes into your
mind. It is time to return to the 'Serving King'. It is the trek with Him
that is your 'home'. It is only in the trek with Him that you feel at 'home'.
Consequences of 'actualities', come what may, will never cause you to
"leave Me alone" again. Welcome home. Trek on...

Day 96
WATCH WITH ME

**Then He said to them, "My soul is very sorrowful, even to death; remain here, and watch with Me."
(Matthew 26:38)**

"We can never fathom the agony in Gethsemane, but at least we need not misunderstand it. It is the agony of God and Man in one, face to face with sin."– Oswald Chambers

Naivety, that blissful state of innocence, in which the child trekking after the King remains clueless concerning the 'price' of salvation, allowing the child to 'sleep' while the 'King' agonizes. It is not a lack of concern, nor a lack of desire to "watch with Me," nor an unwillingness to tarry with the King; instead, it is simply a 'naivety' rooted in ignorance concerning the reality of what is about to unfold.

It is that innocence, that lack of seeing, often preventing the child of the King from genuinely engaging in the 'hard work' of "watch with Me" for the 'hand of God' bringing about the purposes of God in the midst of the myriad of seemingly insignificant details ushering in the reality of your existence. The significance of the solitary man, engaged in the battle of His life, the battle for the 'life' of those who would be impacted by His success, is lost to the vision of those assigned to "watch with Me." To those intended 'watchers', this watch was not different from the hundred previous 'watches' in which Jesus 'worked alone' in the 'hard work of intercessory prayer' while the watchers slept.

Tragically, you, too, will rarely 'see' the significance of the 'hard work' that must be done in intercessory prayer, and not 'seeing' the cruciality of this 'watching in prayer' for those fighting the battle of their lives, you, too, will drift into 'sleep', leaving the battle of a lifetime to be fought alone by those who need most this careful "watch with Me." Somewhere into the trek after the King, you will begin to lose that precious 'naivety' tallowing you to sleep peacefully as the battle rages for others. It is then, and only then, that "watch with Me" will become a significant part of your everyday life. It is then that Jesus will no longer intercede alone for those He watches. The child of the King finally understands the utter importance of "watch with Me" and joins Him in the 'hard work'.

Day 97

THE INTENTIONALITY OF YOUR CROSS

**He Himself bore our sins in His body on the tree, that we might die to sin and live to righteousness.
(1 Peter 2:24)**

"The Cross did not happen to Jesus: He came on purpose for it. He is 'the Lamb slain from the foundation of the world'. The whole meaning of the Incarnation is the Cross."– Oswald Chambers

Those who trek close to the 'Serving King' will soon discover 'random chance', that catchall for the chaos erupting around Him, and consequently those who trek closely with Him, is not nearly so 'random' as one might initially believe. To the contrary, those who begin to 'see' more clearly, will begin to understand that life, even your life, is full of intentionality; perhaps, more intentionality than you will be comfortable with. That, of course, means the child trekking after the Serving King will begin to realize 'life did not happen to Jesus', even as "the cross did not happen to Jesus." Rather, "He came on purpose for it." That creates an immense crisis for the child intent on mimicking the King. Will you 'come on purpose for it'?

Of course, the 'cross', for the child trekking after the King, is rarely the kind to which you will be nailed; instead, it is almost always the 'head on' collision with sin and its claim upon you. But, because sin is so deeply and intricately interwoven into your being, the challenge "that we might die to sin" will usher in a level of suffering like unto death. And like the King, you must determine to be "on purpose for it," to seize the opportunity when it arrives, to 'battle sin' to the death.

Like 'incarnation', it is the 'indwelling presence of the Holy Spirit' enabling the battle with 'sin' to finally occur, even to the point of death. Be prepared for an agonizing endeavor, for 'sin' will not go 'quietly into the night'; rather, it will rage against the Spirit of God in you until the Spirit has vanquished sin, rendering it powerless (Romans 6:6). It is in the midst of that battle that you will finally understand Jesus' plea, "Watch with Me..." (Matthew 26:28). You, too, will join Him in calling those who trek with you to 'watch with Me for my soul is sorrowful', as the battle with sin rages deep into the night, even unto death. You must 'come on purpose for it'. It is for that very moment that God's vision for you, 'from the foundations of the world', finally comes into being.

Day 98

NO TIME TO WASTE

And as they were coming down the mountain, He charged them to tell no one what they had seen, until the Son of Man had risen from the dead.
(Mark 9:9)

"Say nothing until the Son of Man is risen in you–until the life of the risen Christ so dominates you that you understand what the historic Christ taught. When you get to the right state on the inside, the word which Jesus has spoken is so plain that you are amazed you did not see it before. You could not understand it before, you were not in the place in disposition where it could be borne."– Oswald Chambers

Inevitably, the child trekking after the King will 'see' and 'hear' more than they can possibly understand. It is simply the normative consequence for those who trek closely with Jesus. Thus, much of what will be 'seen' and 'heard' will not be comprehended, especially in those early days of the trek. Still, Jesus continues to 'show' you things that cannot be understood causing you to wonder why He continues to 'show' me that which I cannot understand nor talk about?

The simple reality is there is no time to waste in the process of trekking closely with Jesus. Thus, He will grab every available moment to teach you and move you toward completion, along toward maturity, even if those moments can be no more than storing data for later usage.

When the "right state on the inside" finally occurs, an amazing sequence of events begins to unfold as the 'stored but not understood' suddenly becomes crystal clear, one 'domino' after another, the wisdom of God falling in line piece after piece, block by block. The stunning clarity of understanding will indeed cause you to pause, "amazed that you did not see it before." Then the flash of insight, the moment of understanding, the unmistakable clarity concerning the 'why' of your lack of understanding. Previous moments, embedded with a lack of understanding, were linked to an inappropriate condition or disposition; hence, present moment's 'lack of understanding' must also be the by-product of a 'disposition' that is not right. Then you realize the utter importance of making sure that your 'disposition', that embracing obedience, remains the condition of the 'inner being' from that moment onward.

Day 99
NO SHORTCUTS

**"...was it not necessary that the Christ should suffer
these things and enter into His glory?"
(Luke 24:26)**

*"Our Lord's Cross is the gateway into His life: His Resurrection
means that He has power now to convey His life to me. When
I am born again from above, I receive from the risen Lord His
very life. Our Lord's Resurrection destiny is to bring 'many
sons unto glory.'"– Oswald Chambers*

Some trekking after the Serving King seek to find 'shortcuts' to the 'glory', the resurrected life ushering in victory over sin. Indeed, resurrection is testimony not only of the 'salvation' that is to come, but, additionally, the victorious life that can be seized in the present moment. The 'shortcuts', good, in and of themselves, come in many forms of worship, bible reading, service, etc. Each must be heartily engaged in its own way. But these cannot finish the job.

Alas, there is no 'shortcut, no way of by-passing the 'suffering' necessary to enter into the resurrected life He "has the power to convey to me." Thus, the unwillingness to suffer will hinder in the most radical way those who desire to have the resurrected life conveyed to them by the resurrected Lord. It is not that the suffering cannot be avoided, for it easily can; rather, suffering must not be avoided, if a desire is present to be one of these "many sons unto glory." Jesus does not mandate suffering; instead, He simply offers it to the children who truly trek after Him.

The gross sins, those heinous ones that you are glad to be rid of, go painlessly as you toss them to the gutter, delighted to be rid of them. The death of these sins will bring no suffering. No, you will cheer their detaching from your being. However, the sin that clings to you deep into the journey, sin you secretly hold tight, seemingly cannot be laid down; or, more to the point, cannot be torn from you without 'suffering'. It will take the 'power of Christ' to rip secret sins' entrails from you, imbedded deep within the members of your body and being (Romans 7:23). But you simply cannot experience the 'power of the resurrected life' without first enduring the 'pain of suffering', as, at last, these old friends, those sins which have traveled long with you, are torn asunder by the 'power of Christ'. There are no shortcuts. Lie still and let Him "convey His life," the resurrected life, unto you.

Day 100

SEEING JESUS

After these things He appeared in another form to two of them, as they were walking into the country. And they went back and told the rest, but they did not believe them.
Mark 16:12-13

"Being saved and seeing Jesus are not the same thing. Many are partakers of God's grace who have never seen Jesus. When once you have seen Jesus, you can never be the same... Jesus must appear to your friend as well as to you; no one can see Jesus with your eyes. Severance takes place where one and not the other has seen Jesus."– Oswald Chambers

Those so bold as to trek after the Serving King have a tendency to be those who have 'seen' Jesus, rather than those who have simply heard the testimony of peers who have seen Jesus. This is no small distinction. The privilege of having 'seen' Jesus cannot be manufactured, try as one might. Rather, Jesus must make Himself 'known', become visible, to those whom He intends to follow Him in the closest manner possible, those who 'trek' after Him. You will be tempted to think, "I will see Him if I remain in the company of those who have 'seen' Him, but rarely will Jesus make Himself known to you in the 'company of the many'; rather, it is 'another form' in which Jesus typically appears. This 'another form' varies from person to person, often unique, suited precisely for each distinctive journey.

'Having seen' Jesus, while an incredibly transformative experience, launching many a follower into the trek, will not be enough to 'sustain' the trekker over the course of a lifetime. Lifetime trekkers have not simply 'seen' Jesus, rather they 'see' Jesus on a day by day basis. It is the daily encounter with the Risen Lord that invigorates the trekker for the lifelong journey. It is that daily 'walk into the country' with Jesus providing insight and clarity for each day's trek.

Be not dismayed when others cannot believe what you 'see', nor understand the trek you must take. It has always been this way, "and they went back and told the rest, but they did not believe them." A friend cannot see and hear through your eyes and ears. It is in your 'witness' of what you see and hear that allows the 'many in the company of others' to search for that 'walk into the country' that each trekker must take, if they are to experience the joy of 'seeing and hearing' Jesus.

Day 101
CRUCIFIED OR DEAD?

We know that our old self was crucified with Him in order that the body of sin might be brought to nothing, so that we would no longer be enslaved to sin.
(Romans 6:6)

"It takes a long time to come to a moral decision about sin, but it is the great moment in my life when I do decide that just as Jesus Christ died for the sin of the world, so sin must die out in me, not be curbed or suppressed or counteracted, but crucified. No one can bring anyone else to this decision."–
Oswald Chambers

Crucifixion is never a quick and painless process; to the contrary, it is a very long and tedious experience, and therein lies the problem for the child trekking after the Serving King. The crucifixion of Jesus was not the norm with its quickened death. Rather than being nailed to a cross, most victims of crucifixion were simply tied to a stake, left to hang days on end, dying a very slow and agonizing death, culminating in suffocation as the utterly exhausted body, deprived of all water and nutrients, failed to find strength to flex the muscles surrounding the lungs, enabling air to provide the needed oxygen for the body. Thus, in the end, the victim suffocates in the most agonizing manner possible.

So must be the crucifixion of the 'old self', as it is robbed of all sustenance enabling it to survive. Oh, how 'little' sustenance the 'old self' needs to survive. The 'old self' will beg and plead for mercy as it hangs helplessly, isolated in a chamber of the heart, deep within the 'being' of the child trekking after the King. You will be tempted to be merciful and gracious, allowing it to remain in its weakened condition, feeding it just enough to sustain its feeble state, thinking it to be harmless, weakened and crucified, hanging so helplessly. However, the 'crucifixion' itself is not the intended end. No, 'death' is the intended end, the culminating goal of crucifixion.

The child trekking after the King will need to be very careful not to feed or water the 'old self'. Just the slightest nutrition, one bad attitude, one lustful thought, one moment of anger, jealously or strife will keep the 'old self' sustained for weeks on end. Crucifixion must end in death, "that the body of sin might be brought to nothing." It is only when the 'old self' has died that the child trekking after the King can proclaim, "we would no longer be enslaved to sin."

Day 102

AN INFUSION OF A DIFFERENT KIND

**For if we have been united with Him in a death like His, we shall certainly be united with Him in a resurrection like His.
(Romans 6:5)**

"The incoming of the Spirit of Jesus into me readjusts my personal life to God. The resurrection of Jesus has given Him authority to impart the life of God to me...the resurrection life of Jesus invades every bit of my human nature."– Oswald Chambers

The 'invasion' of the resurrected life of Jesus into "every bit of my human nature" can be a bit overwhelming for the child trekking after the Serving King; for it is indeed an invasion of the most pervasive kind, streaming into every nook and cranny of your being. It is only then, in the moment of invasion, the full extent of the intent of the resurrected Christ really becomes clear, as His Spirit begins to claim 'authority' in each area of the 'reclaimed heart'. The sudden empowerment, the ability to conquer age-old strongholds of sin, some insignificant, others crippling the trekking child over the span of many years, creates a serious 'readjusts my personal life to God'.

Thus, the 'readjustments of my personal life' begin to take shape are much more comprehensive and extensive than could have been initially imagined. Those comfortable boundaries in which the Spirit of the resurrected Christ 'played nice' with the desires of the self are suddenly obliterated, as the power of the living Spirit barges into previously closed dimensions of 'personal life'. But once the 'old self' has been crucified (Romans 6:6), the walls of protection, built and sustained by the 'old self', crumble easily at the feet of the conquering Spirit.

As those 'walls' crumble, "the resurrected life of Jesus invades every bit of my human nature," cleansing, purifying, bleaching with every touch of the Spirit, rendering afresh spirit and nature, empowering with the 'imparted life of God'. Thus, this dying of the 'old self' is merely the footstool for the 'imparted life of God', that radical transformation of 'being', rendering the child trekking after the King a 'new creation', imparted with the 'life of God', free from the 'power of sin'. It is then, and only then, that the child of the King can 'obey', 'walking as He walked'. This is an "infusion of a different kind" and the 'trek after the Serving King' will never be the same.

Day 103
DEAD TO COZY SIN?

...death no longer has dominion over Him. For the death He died He died to sin, once for all, but the life He lives He lives to God. So you also must consider yourselves dead to sin and alive to God in Christ Jesus.
(Romans 6:9-11)

"The energy and the power which were manifested in Jesus will be manifested in us by the sheer sovereign grace of God when once we have made the moral decision about sin."– Oswald Chambers

The partnership with sin, at least the ongoing partnership with the 'lesser sins', those shortcomings seemingly harmless enough, is an exceedingly difficult partnership to break. The vile sins, those outrageous and flagrant shortcomings, have long been surrendered, left behind in the early days of the trek alongside Jesus. The 'lesser sins', however, those cozy friends hidden in the cellar of the heart, shielded from the cleansing power of the Spirit, continue to woo the heart, cozying up to the 'inner being', providing an awkward comfort in 'fallenness', beckoning unto the grace of God to provide shelter in the 'inner being' of the child trekking after the King. It is an awkward partnership proving difficult to sever regardless of 'good intentions'.

Thus, the 'moral decision' about 'cozy sin' is often very late in the trek, only when the trekker begins to understand the pace of Jesus is exceeding the pace that can be sustained while weighted down by the heaviness of 'cozy sin' continuing to linger in the inner being. It is that moment of 'awareness' that a "moral decision about sin" must be made, a final declaration that 'all sin', even the 'cozy sin', must be 'dead to you', done away with, once and for all.

It is in that final 'moral decision about sin' that the "energy and power" of Jesus begin to manifest as the partnership with 'cozy sin' is finally severed in a radical way, rendering you free to 'trek' side by side with Jesus, "alive to God." The 'manifested power' exercises dominion over the 'cozy sin' as each 'cozy sin' is cast aside, moment by moment, day by day, month after month, freeing the child to an obedience only possible when 'sin' has been conquered, vanquished, squelched and left to die a lonely death as the child trekking after the King walks quickly away from the castaway of 'cozy sin', an old friend who once held so great sway. Only the child who truly "consider yourselves dead to sin" can exercise this kind of 'power'.

111

Day 104

CASTING BURDENS

Cast your burden on the Lord, and He will sustain you.
(Psalm 55:22)

"Many workers have gone out with high courage and fine impulses, but with no intimate fellowship with Jesus Christ, and before long they are crushed. They do not know what to do with the burden, it produces weariness, and people say– 'What an embittered end to such a beginning!'"– Oswald Chambers

Trekking after the Serving King is rarely engaged in by those who lack 'high courage and fine impulses'; to the contrary, almost to a person, they will have exemplary courage and impulses. 'High courage and fine impulses' will indeed send a child of the King into the field of service, but no child can be sustained in the field without a genuine and deep personal relationship with the Serving King. Still, countless trekkers have been found exhausted and discouraged, buried under the burden of the needs of those who clamor for the attention of those who trek after the Serving King.

You will be tempted to pick up the load of others who provide great emotional rewards through praise and thanksgiving, some directed at you, some directed at Jesus, but you will, sooner rather than later, discover the high cost of this praise is not compensated by the reward you receive from those delighted to let you carry their loads. They will delight in your willingness to carry each and any burden. Cheer you on they will.

In that moment of realization, you will be tempted to cast that load back onto the back of those who gleefully gave it you, but that will do no good, for you really do 'care' about those whom you were trying to assist. The burden would be twice as heavy if you went back a second time to assist those in need. So instead, cast 'your burden', the burden you have taken from others and claimed as your own, onto the Lord. Ultimately, it is only Jesus, the actual Savior, Who can carry the load of the many. That is a reality you will have to get used to somewhere along the journey.

Only Jesus with His infinite wisdom and strength can carry a load like this. Resist the temptation to pick it up; instead, 'cast your burden on the Lord, and He will sustain you' and those whom you care most about. Recognize your limitation long before the load crushes you.

Day 105

A DIFFERENT KIND OF YOKE

"Take My yoke upon you, and learn from Me..."
(Matthew 11:29)

"'Whom the Lord loveth, He chasteneth.' How petty our complaining is! Our Lord begins to bring us into the place where we can have communion with Him, and we groan and say– 'Oh Lord, let me be like other people!' Jesus is asking us to take one end of the yoke– 'My yoke is easy, get alongside Me and we will pull together.'"– Oswald Chambers

It is a sobering reality when the child trekking after the King suddenly hears the suggestion, rather command, to pick up the yoke of the Serving King. But understand this 'picking up of the yoke' is not to assist Jesus in pulling the load; rather, it is to learn how to walk as Jesus, to pull the load. It is important to comprehend what this 'yoke' actually is. Simply, it is 'learning' to think and act as Jesus thinks and acts.

It is in learning to think and act like Jesus that you will be tempted to say, "Oh Lord, let me be like other people!" However, Jesus is not like other people nor will He allow those who are 'yoked' with Him to be like other people. You cannot walk 'yoked' to the Jesus and walk any way but His. That is the whole purpose of the 'yoke' as the two must function as one. You must learn His cadence and pace. It is in the experience of 'yokedness' that you discover in an even more profound way, His ways are not your ways.

Yet, Jesus is forthright in reminding the child trekking after the King that His way of 'being and doing' is not difficult; to the contrary, "For my yoke is easy and My burden is light" (Matthew 11:30). But, and this is critical to understand, His way is different, radically different, than how you have lived before. You will be tempted to suggest 'different' is hard, burdensome and problematic for you. It is not. His way is simply different. A decision will have to be made. Will you stay 'yoked' to Jesus?

Then, some days into 'yokedness', that moment of blissful discovery as you remain in His yoke, walking with Him, side by side, His way instead of your way, mile after mile, He is carrying the burden. Then, you understand His concept of 'shared yoke' is nothing like yours. His way is to carry the burden while you walk and learn. Stay yoked and walk on.

Day 106

PURITY OF HEART IS NOT ENOUGH

**But the high places were not taken out of Israel. Nevertheless, the heart of Asa was wholly true all his days.
(2 Chronicles 15:17)**

"You are all right in the main, but you are slipshod; there is a relapse on the line of concentration. You no more need a holiday from spiritual concentration than your heart needs a holiday from beating."– Oswald Chambers

For the child trekking after the Serving King, a lackadaisical attitude can develop, even while the heart remains 'wholly true'. King Asa discovered 'purity of heart' was not enough in the end, for the God of Israel whose standards extend beyond the 'simplicity of a pure heart', deep into the actual ways of 'being and doing'. You will be tempted to think God is content with the 'purity of your heart', but God's standards extend way beyond the 'heart', into the realm of how life is actually lived. That will take some getting used to.

It is only when walking in the yoke of Jesus, one begins to understand 'purity of heart' is not the ultimate goal, critical as the 'heart' is to God. Rather, 'purity of heart' is the foundation out of which life springs, but life must still be shaped and guided by 'wisdom', that 'way of life' (how life is actually lived) God intends for God's children. Hence, the call of Jesus to "take my yoke and learn from me" (Matthew 11:29). This way of life must be learned; it does not flow naturally from even a 'wholly true' heart. The unlearned, even those whose hearts are 'wholly true', will live in a manner displeasing to God, if their actual 'doing' is not guided by the 'wisdom of God', the 'way' God intends for things to be done.

Thus, the child intent on not only trekking after the King, but trekking in 'the way' God intends, will have to commit to learning how God intends for 'this or that' to be done. Be not surprised that God has a 'way' for every 'this or that'. King Asa forgot that the 'this or that' mattered and, of course, there were unintended consequences for not only himself but for those whom he led. Never assume your 'pure heart' is producing the right 'way' of 'this or that'. Learn how God intends for each and every 'this or that' to be done. There is an intended way to do every 'this or that'.

Day 107

SEIZE THE LIGHT WHILE YOU CAN

"While you have the Light, believe in the Light, that you may become sons of Light."
(John 12:36)

"Those moments are moments of insight which we have to live up to when we do not feel like it... We have to learn to live in the grey day according to what we saw on the mount."–Oswald Chambers

Moments of insight, 'light', are so very precious. For the child trekking after the Serving King who has taken up the 'yoke' of Christ, learning as He teaches along the trek (Matthew 11:29), it will seem that the 'light' is constantly on, ever-present, endlessly effervescent. But Jesus reminds us this 'light' will not last forever, ever burning, ever- present. No, 'light' will come and go, as Jesus dictates.

The 'light' is not random; rather, it comes as Jesus intends, ready for immediate application, ready to be believed, ready to be actualized. You will want to stay in the 'light', learning the particulars of additional 'this and that', but Jesus does not teach in that way. Instead, this 'light' comes in the 'moments of insight' that must find expression before additional 'light' will be provided. 'Light' is never meant to be simply principles and theory; rather, it is merely the foundation out of which action must arise. It is not those who 'have the light' who are 'sons of light'; rather, it is those who 'believe' by 'doing' and so 'become sons of light'.

Never assume that the 'light', even 'light' that has been given previously, will always be available. It simply will not. Thus, never miss an opportunity to seize the 'light' when it is shining. Those who do will soon discover there is much to be learned by those who have taken the opportunity to pick up the yoke of Jesus. It is a rare privilege to walk closely with the 'light'. Seize the opportunity while the light is on.

Day 108
SEIZE THE LIGHT NOW

**When Simon Peter heard that it was the Lord, he put on
his outer garment, for he was stripped for work,
and threw himself into the sea.
(John 21:7)**

*"Have you ever had a crisis in which you deliberately and
emphatically and recklessly abandoned everything?"– Oswald
Chambers*

Peter, three years into his trek after Jesus, learned to 'seize the light' (John 12:36) while it could be seized; hence, his radical impatience to wait for the fishing boat to return to shore. He knew in the most profound way possible, having abandoned Jesus during the chaos of His trial and execution, the 'light of Jesus' would not be available just because he called into the night, and he determined not to miss a single moment of this 'here again light'; even if it meant leaving behind other things, important things, things needing to be done. Peter determined to 'seize the light' right then, less he risk Jesus exiting again.

There is a great lesson for the child trekking after the Serving King that ought not to be missed by those who encounter Peter's reckless abandonment. When the 'light appears', and it will appear at the most seemingly inappropriate times, drop everything to get to the 'light' before it is gone. This is a difficult lesson for all to learn, for indeed 'light' often appears when there are many other important things going on around you. Those things will need to be dropped as you charge ahead to 'seize' the light available now, right now, convenient or not.

But it is not just the light from Jesus that ought to be seized, it is light coming from a variety of sources, parents, teachers, pastors, etc. You will be tempted to take for granted that you can learn from them tomorrow, but many tomorrows will never come and countless opportunities are vanquished at the feet of foolish decisions to 'stay in the boat' just a little longer. Resist the temptation to fish a little longer. Grab your garments and plunge into the water. Go ahead, "deliberately and emphatically and recklessly abandon everything" to seize the light, wisdom, while it can be found. Understand that many, if not most, other 'trekkers' will stay in the safety of the boat, waiting till it is convenient to 'seize the light'. They will not risk the plunge with you. This is a trek that will often unfold in isolation. Worry not, jump in while the 'light' is still shining.

Day 109

SEIZE THE LIGHT NOW

God called to him out of the bush, "Moses, Moses!"
And he said, "Here I am."
(Exodus 3:4)

"Be ready for the sudden surprise visits of God. A ready person never needs to get ready. Think of the time we waste trying to get ready when God has called!"—Oswald Chambers

The 'light' (John 12:36) often shows up in the most unexpected places and times. Moses is not the first to discover God's penchant for popping up in the most ordinary and mundane places to announce the most extraordinary and incredible 'callings' concerning your life. Those trekking after the Serving King, accustomed to God speaking in those expected and normal ways, sitting in the pew, relaxing over coffee in the living room, will often miss these 'out of the bush' moments in which God manifests in the most extraordinary ways.

But the call of Moses is not unique. God will often beckon unto you from the 'bush' in your backyard, but you will only hear God if you have learned to listen for God's voice in the midst of your day-to-day activities. This listening in the midst of the mundane is a learned art you will want to master. Like Peter (John 21:7), and now Moses, you will have to drop whatever it is that you are doing, important as your 'tending sheep' may be, and approach that 'talking bush' for further details.

The first step is utterly important for further communication to occur, "Here I am." It is in the simple acknowledgement of the presence of God that He then begins to engage in those most extraordinary conversations about the future of your life. You will think it odd God has chosen to communicate this extraordinary vision for your life in the most mundane place and time. Mundane is simply how God often speaks to those He intends to use in the most significant ways. You will soon discover the presence of the 'Living God' turns even the Playland at McDonalds into the most sacred of places.

If, like Moses, God asks you to remove your shoes in the middle of the McDonalds Playland, know that you are entering sacred ground in the midst of all the ordinary chaos life often throws at you. Church buildings rarely provide this most intimate of conversations with God. Trek on...

Day 110

THE DANGER OF FINISHING POORLY

**...for Joab had supported Adonijah although he had not sup-
ported Absalom – Joab fled to the tent of the Lord and
caught hold of the horns of the altar.
(I Kings 2:28)**

*"We are apt to say – 'It is not in the least likely that having been
through the supreme crisis, I shall turn now to the things of
the world.' Do not forecast where the temptation will come; it
is the least likely thing that is the peril."– Oswald Chambers*

Faithfulness in the moment, even in lots of moments, does not ensure faithfulness in all moments, or the crucial moments awaiting us as we approach the finish line. Joab, faithful to David on so many occasions, most notably in the battle against Absalom, the young and handsome son of David attempting to overthrow David's throne, surrendered his faithfulness to David late in life. Like so many of us, his faithfulness waned because he felt David had not honored him properly late into the journey with David (2 Samuel 20:1-13). A root of bitterness springs so easily in the life of those long into the trek after the Serving King.

For the child trekking after the Serving King, late failures often occur precisely under those same circumstances, a frustration the King has not honored you properly in consideration of years of faithful service. The erosion of faithfulness rarely occurs in that sudden collapse; rather, a steady erosion slowly depleting loyalty, almost unnoticeable in the early stages, while nonetheless real. Further, it is not typically the 'supreme crisis' producing failure, but rather, that 'least likely thing' produces great peril to the life of faith. It is the little failures that undermine finishing well.

Thus, it becomes critical to never allow a slow-burning bitterness and frustration toward the King to quietly take root in your being. You must face the reality that the King inevitably will call you to areas of service you deem unworthy of your station. The reward you deem 'yours' goes to another (Amasa), leaving you frustrated and suspect to failures in 'the least likely thing'. Joab is not unique, nor even unusual. He, like so many before and after him, finished poorly. Be on your guard. Yesterday's successes will not carry the need of the present moment. Run the good race. Finish well.

Day 111
THE AMEN TO GOD

**For all the promises of God find their Yes in Him. That is why it is through Him that we utter our, "Amen to God for His glory."
(2 Corinthians 1:20)**

"When it is a question of God's Almighty Spirit, never say 'I can't.' Never let the limitation of natural ability come in. If we have received the Holy Spirit, God expects the work of the Holy Spirit to be manifested in us...Never forget that our capacity in spiritual matters is measured by the promises of God."– Oswald Chambers

For the child trekking after the Serving King, learning to "utter our Amen to God" is not an easy thing. The 'Amen', taken for granted as a conclusion to prayers of all kinds, has lost its meaning, rendering its declaration of 'make it so' or 'true' as null and void in far too many instances. But the 'Amen to God' has greater significance for those who begin to hear the promises of significance from the 'burning bush' (Exodus 3:4).

Still, like Moses, too many children trekking after the King will hear the 'promises of God' and negate the very things God has declared He will do. The negation, rooted in the pride of humility, nestled in the self-awareness of inability, protecting the self from the promises of God, renders the trekker useless. However, the promises of God, uttered in the midst of the mundane circumstances of life and the very real inabilities of the trekker, have no need for abilities and skills of the trekker; to the contrary, the promises of God are rooted in the very being of God, the character and nature of God, the empowering only God can provide. Hence, the trekker need not worry about self-limitations, for God never intended to use the abilities of the trekker. The promises of God are dependent upon God and God alone.

The trekker, upon hearing the promises of God, the declarations of God, need only say, "Amen to God." The trekker need only say, "Make it so, Lord." It is the capacity of God empowering the trekker to attain the promises of God. All the trekker need do is believe God can and will do what God has promised He will do. Learn the cadence of those who trek alongside the Serving King, "Make it so, Lord. Amen!"

Day 112

DO YOU ASTOUND HIM?

**"Have I been with you so long, and you still
do not know Me, Philip?"
(John 14:9)**

*"Our Lord must be repeatedly astounded at us..."– Oswald
Chambers*

Deep into the trek after the Serving King, you will begin to relax in your pursuit, thinking you 'know' Him. Indeed, in many ways you do. But the depth of Jesus and the limits to what you can understand at each step of the journey, try as you may, will render Jesus 'unknowable' in many ways in each present moment. That can be discouraging for a child trekking after the Serving King.

However, it also can provide a lifetime of discovery for the trekker who continues to search deep into the nature and being of Jesus. Each day will bring fresh insight, and it is that daily insight into the being of Jesus keeping the relationship fresh and ever life-changing. It is the vastness of His being ushering in an ever expanding knowledge of Who Jesus really is. Don't be discouraged by how much there is yet to discover about Jesus. That is one of the great serendipitous aspects of the journey.

However, never confuse the 'yet unknown' with what can be 'known' or, better yet, what should be known. There is a vast difference between the two. The former, arising out of the depth of Who Jesus is and the limited number of days you have spent with Him. The latter, those things that should be known, create a great number of "our Lord must be repeatedly astounded at us." Philip, in the midst of learning more about Who and What Jesus is, suddenly discovers he has missed an important foundation stone of 'knowing Jesus'. He astounds Jesus with how little he has absorbed. "Philip, have I been with you so long, and you still do not know Me?"

Should you discover you are not receiving fresh and invigorating insights into the nature and being of Jesus, chances are you have not understood an essential piece previously offered. Go back and review what has been shared previously. There is a foundation stone of knowledge you failed to grasp, putting tomorrow's insights on hold until you do. Be careful not to 'astound' Jesus. Go back and find that missing bit of 'knowing'.

Day 113
SEEING THOUGH THE VEIL?

**And we all, with unveiled face, beholding the glory of the Lord, are being transformed into the same image from one degree of glory to another.
(2 Corinthians 3:18)**

"Allow nothing to keep you from looking God sternly in the face about yourself and about your doctrine, and every time you preach see that you look God in the face about things first, then the glory will remain all through."–Oswald Chambers

Rarely, if ever, does a child trekking after the King enter into the presence of God with unveiled face. It simply is not the normative way of 'being and doing', try as we might; instead, most are masters at wearing the 'veil', as if God cannot see directly through any and every kind of veil. Nonetheless, there is simply too much to hide, too much remains buried within to approach the 'glory of the Lord' with unveiled face; or so we think. Learning to approach God with an 'unveiled face' will take some time before finally becoming a way of life. In the meantime, the 'veil' unintentionally clouds our ability to see the 'glory of the Lord', hampered, as vision through a 'veil' must always be.

That, of course, is the problem with our 'veils', those shallow attempts to prevent God from seeing the 'real' you. Those protective 'veils', useless as they may be in hindering the 'vision' of God, are problematic for the child who continues to wear them. The 'veil' hinders the vision of the child attempting to 'behold the glory of God'. It is the 'glory of the Lord' that 'transforms' those who see it into the 'same image' of the Living God. Hence, your transformation cannot occur until you remove the 'veil', all the 'veils'; those transparent efforts to conceal what is real, buried deep within.

Thus, the discovery of that unknown hindrance preventing the transformation you so desire. The veil, in all its forms, must come off, enabling you to finally see the 'glory of the Lord' and its transformative power in the life of those who have 'seen the glory of the Lord'. Don't be naive, God has known the 'real' you all along. Be not surprised when the 'veil' is finally removed and you discover the 'real' you as well. Trek on...

Day 114

THE DISTRACTION OF GODLY WORK

For we are God's fellow workers.
(1 Corinthians 3:9)

"Beware of any work for God which enables you to evade concentration on Him. A great many Christian workers worship their work."– Oswald Chambers

The honor and glory of trekking with the Serving King provides an abundance of self-worth. Of more value yet is the honor of being asked to 'work' with or for the Serving King. But you will want to be very careful about the 'kind' of work you engage in while serving the King. Some work comes with its own rewards, and those rewards, the joy of the task itself, the praise of others, the profit, etc., will, in and of themselves, distract you from keeping your attention and focus on the 'working' God. Soon, the task itself becomes the reward.

You may discover you love the 'work' of God more than you love God. Loving the 'work' of God more than you love God will ultimately crush your ability to stay in intimate fellowship with God, and those who lose fellowship with God will ultimately fall out of love with God. Thus, every Christian worker will have to pause and ask, "Does this task I love hinder my ability to remain focused on God?" If the answer is yes, you will have to surrender that task, even if it was originally assigned by God, because it has become a distraction to your relationship with God.

In that moment, resist the temptation to say, "But I am doing God's work and that must be a good thing." No work remains 'good' if it distracts you from your relationship with God or your ability to stay focused on God. In the end, that which was intended for 'good', the very task God assigned, has become displeasing to God, pulling you farther and farther from the God Whom you seek to serve in the task at hand. You must surrender that task quickly, and refocus your attention completely and fully on God, allowing that relationship to rekindle in all of its fullness.

Fear not, there will be many days ahead with all kinds of tasks needing to be done. But in the moment of the 'distraction of Godly work', abandon that task and return to simply 'trekking with the King'. Don't allow any task to replace intimate fellowship with God as you trek on.

Day 115
THE DANGER OF COMMERCIALISM

"Nevertheless, do not rejoice in this, that the spirits are subject to you, but rejoice that your names are written in heaven."
(Luke 10:20)

"Jesus told the disciples not to rejoice in successful service, and yet this seems to be the one thing in which most of us do rejoice. We have the commercial view–so many souls saved and sanctified, thank God, now it is all right."– Oswald Chambers

More dangerous to a 'heart after God' distracted by a love of 'God's work', maybe success in the task God has assigned or 'The Danger of Commercialism'. The danger arises in the subtle forms as the child trekking after the Serving King begins to crave the sense of accomplishment accompanying success, a success in the most important of all tasks, the redemption of 'souls'. Especially when God has proclaimed in the early days of success, "Job well done, good and faithful servant!" The thrill of success goes beyond description.

This becomes even more problematic as those 'saved souls' begin to sing your praises, all in the form of praises to God, but nonetheless striking a chord of accomplishment deep within your soul. It is in those moments you must turn your attention toward God, and God alone; else, you will soon discover how easily the praise of God can be drowned out by the praise of 'saved souls'. And how equally fast the 'ear' soon begins to tune itself to the praise of those who have genuinely experienced the redemption God has made possible through you. There is great rejoicing in the discovery "spirits are subject to you."

Follow the instruction of Jesus and resist the temptation to celebrate, especially with others, the successes God brings. Instead, rejoice with God, and God alone. Tune your ear to God's praise and resist the temptation to join in the celebration of those who have found redemption in Christ. It is in the moment of success that you must be on your guard to protect yourself from a spirit of 'commercialism' that will ultimately chip away at the foundation of a relationship with God. Beware the danger of success in the things of God. Trek on tuned only to the praise of the King.

Day 116
THE VALLEY OF NORMALCY

**...preach the word; be ready in season and out of season; reprove, rebuke, and exhort, with complete patience and teaching.
(2 Timothy 2:4)**

"There are unemployables in the spiritual domain, spiritually decrepit people, who refuse to do anything unless they are supernaturally inspired. The proof that we are rightly related to God is that we do our best whether we feel inspired or not."– Oswald Chambers

For the child trekking after the Serving King, there will indeed be 'mountaintop' moments in which the vitality of the relationship with God is so intense inspiration flows in the most profound ways. You will be sorely tempted to stay in that 'mountaintop' moment, but you cannot, God never allows it. Every child begins to sense the 'mountaintop' is moving away, and you will try to chase it, find it again, but alas, the 'mountaintop' only appears when God deems it necessary for a wide variety of reasons you cannot access nor predict.

When the 'mountaintop' has moved on and the child returns to the 'valley of normalcy', a decision must be made about how to approach life in the 'valley of normalcy', those long periods of time when you do not sense the heightened immediacy of the Holy Spirit, and yet life continues to roll right along. You will be tempted to refrain from the tasks that God has called you to, declaring you can only engage when the 'Spirit moves you', but that simply is not the case. Instead, you must be ready to engage with your very best, regardless of the 'season' you are in, and yes, the season is about you, not the external conditions surrounding you.

Consider the reality that God has prepared you for the 'valley of normalcy' and has rendered you capable, even without the 'heightened immediacy' of the Holy Spirit you deem essential to engagement. Recognize God has done a work in you rendering you ready to engage, 'in season and out of season'. God has prepared you to 'trek on' in the 'valley of normalcy', fully engaged with the resources God has provided and left with you during those 'mountaintop' experiences. Be what you have been called to be in the 'valley of normalcy'. When you need the 'mountaintop' again, God will provide at precisely the right moment. In the meantime, trek on.

Day 117
THE SHOCKING COMMAND

"Take your son, your only son Isaac, whom you love, and go to the land of Moriah, and offer him there as a burnt offering on one of the mountains of which I shall tell you."
(Genesis 2:22)

"The great point of Abraham's faith in God was that he was prepared to do anything for God. He was there to obey God, no matter to what belief he went contrary. Abraham was not a devotee of his convictions..."– Oswald Chambers

Sooner or later, for every child trekking after the Serving King, a command comes that shocks and confounds, even for the most devoted child of the King. There is no escaping this simple reality. Eventually, God will shock you with startling commands for your life or, most difficult of all, the life of another. In that moment, you will face the greatest struggle of your entire trek with God, a struggle testing the very limits of your devotion to God, perhaps even your sanity.

The intensity of the struggle will come as the command of God runs contrary to what you have previously believed about the nature and character of God. It will not be that the command simply runs counter to 'reason', but that it challenges your very understanding of Who God is and how God operates within God's creation, how God loves. This will startle you in the most profound way possible. And it will usher in a crisis of intensity that you have not dreamed possible.

In those moments, clarity is critical, essential to moving forward. Abraham's decisive response to the call of God is precisely because he knew it was God Who was calling him to this action, yet seemingly so contrary to the nature of God. You will want that same clarity, certainty it is the calling of God, and not some misunderstanding. If there is the slightest doubt, pause, wait until you know it is from God. But when that moment comes, and come it will, and certainty arrives, hesitate not. Don't expect those of us watching your decision to have the certainty you have. Moments like this are most often strictly between you and God Who has called you. Be prepared for a depth of relationship with God changing your life in the most profound ways possible.

Day 118

MOVING AWAY FROM THINGS

And do you seek great things for yourself?
(Jeremiah 45:5)

"If you have only come the length of asking God for things, you have never come to the first strand of abandonment, you have become a Christian from a standpoint of your own. 'I did ask God for the Holy Spirit, but He did not give me the rest and the peace I expected.' Instantly God puts His finger on the reason—you are not seeking the Lord at all, you are seeking something for yourself."—Oswald Chambers

For a child trekking after the Serving King, it is a difficult moment of self-discovery (enlightenment from God) when the realization of 'expectations' concerning your journey with God becomes self-evident. It is a sobering realization to discover your relationship with God rotates around 'things', important 'things', 'things' needed for life and sustenance, but simply 'things' nonetheless. Even 'great things', 'things' that are of the King's business, often become a distraction to a relationship with the God Who provides all 'things', great and small. An 'expectation' of 'things' can do more harm than you imagine, especially when your 'expectations' are not fulfilled in the time and place you 'expect'.

The 'first strand of abandonment', yes the first, not the last, only comes when you have broken free from the 'expectation' of 'things' and find yourself content, genuinely content, with an ever-deepening dependency and relationship with God. It is in that relationship of dependency upon God that you suddenly discover how few 'things' you really need for life and happiness.

But do not expect your freedom from the need of 'things', even great 'things', to come easily. 'Things' is a way of life for the child trekking after the Serving King, and yet, as the trekking child soon discovers, 'things' temper the speed of the trek. Hence, God in His infinite love for us, begins to slowly tear us away from a dependency on 'things' toward a dependency on God, and God alone. And you will try to persuade God, yourself and others that 'things' are not a distraction toward utter dependency on and with God. But your persuasive words will only persuade you. Turn loose of those 'things' that hinder, even those 'great things'. Trek on...

Day 119
THE PRIZE OF LIFE

"And do you seek great things for yourself? Seek them not, for behold, I am bringing disaster upon all flesh," declares the Lord. "But I will give you your life as a prize of war in all places to which you may go."
(Jeremiah 45:5)

"This is the unshakable secret of the Lord to those who trust Him– 'I will give thee thy life.' What more does a man want than his life? It is the essential thing. 'Thy life for a prey' means that wherever you may go, even if it is into hell, you will come out with your life, nothing can harm it."– Oswald Chambers

The 'unshakeable secret of the Lord' is discovered by all those trekking after the Serving King. But the when of this discovery, the realization 'life' is what really matters, varies greatly from trekker to trekker. Some only discover this truth late in the 'war' (life), when time has ravaged the flesh and stripped it of all pretense of vitality, corrupting it to the point of death, rendering the trekker an invalid, clinging at death's door. In that surreal moment, the trekker suddenly realizes what the writer of Ecclesiastes understood so well, "I have seen everything that is done under the sun, and behold, all is vanity and a striving after wind" (Ecclesiastes 1:14). In the end only 'life' itself can be sustained, and even that, only when in relationship with the One Who can give life is sustained.

Others, the fortunate ones, will learn the 'unshakeable secret of the Lord' much earlier in the trek. To them is granted the privilege of knowing, more to the point, valuing 'life', that intimate recognition only 'life' in relationship to God has any value. In that moment, all the 'things', those sidecars to life consuming our energy, suddenly find their true value: enhancements to a 'life' lived in relationship to the 'Living God'. With that recognition comes the ability to detach from the 'things' won and lost in the 'war', as all trekkers know all too well, the 'war' always ends in 'disaster upon all flesh', sooner or later.

Learn early to value and seize "your life as a prize of war." Those who have 'life' fear no 'war' with all of its ups and downs, gains and loses. 'Life' is the only prize that matters for those trekking after the Serving King.

Day 120
AVOID THE NEST OF CONTENTMENT

Beloved, we are God's children now, and what we will be has not yet appeared...
(1 John 3:2)

"Naturally, we are inclined to be so mathematical and calculating that we look upon uncertainty as a bad thing. We imagine that we have to reach some end, but that is not the nature of spiritual life. The nature of spiritual life is that we are certain in our uncertainty, consequently we do not make our nests anywhere."– Oswald Chambers

Trekking after the Serving King is filled with more uncertainly than we are used to or comfortable with, both in terms of where we are going and what we are to become. Indeed that can be a 'nerve-wracking' condition in the long term. Thus, we have a built-in tendency to 'nest' in the safe place of 'contentment with who and what I am now in Christ'. That 'nest' of contentment provides a safe harbor for life and far too many trekkers will never leave the nest, safe and secure in yesterday's 'becoming'.

However, there are many trekkers who understand God never intends for us to cuddle up in a 'nest' of contentment, free from the drama of 'becoming' all that God has called us to be. Theirs is a journey deeper and deeper into the transformation God intends for those who would trek after God, "but be transformed by the renewal of your mind, that by testing you may discern what is the will of God, what is good and acceptable and perfect" (Romans 12:2). This 'what we will be' of which John speaks is proportional to the 'renewing of the mind' that the trekker enables to occur by ingesting the truth of God's Word and finding ways to apply it in the mundane of day-to-day living.

Therein lies the secret to the 'what will be has not yet appeared'. The 'appearing' only manifests as the trekker begins to 'be and do' what it is the Word is bringing to understanding. But you will be tempted to stay in the comfort of the 'nest', content with the early forms of 'being and doing', never stepping out your comfort zone into the 'what will be' of tomorrow's obedience. Take a moment, look around and examine your 'nest' carefully. Does it look the same today as it did yesterday? Have you simply settled into yesterday's nest and robbed yourself of '...what we will be'? Step out of the 'nest' and transform into what "has not yet appeared."

Day 121
INTENTIONAL SPONTANEITY

Love is patient and kind...
(1 Corinthians 13:4)

"If we try to prove to God how much we love Him, it is a sure sign that we do not love Him. The evidence of our love for Him is the absolute spontaneity of our love, it comes naturally." – Oswald Chambers

Spontaneity, especially 'absolute spontaneity', can be an illusive dimension to a life spent trekking after the Serving King. Some, and they are wrong, will think 'spontaneity' simply springs forth in some uncontrollable and whimsical manner. Nothing could be farther from the truth. Rather, 'absolute spontaneity' arises from a foundation carefully built and sustained by those who desire a 'spontaneous' love toward God.

This 'foundation', carefully crafted and maintained, has key 'bricks' each child must attentively place and sustain if 'spontaneous' love is to arise. The first and critical brick is the 'image' of the Serving King each trekker acquires and stores in the mind. How you 'think' about God, how you 'image' God, will directly impact how you 'spontaneously' feel about God. Thus, the child trekking after the King will want to carefully 'image' God in the most positive light possible. Thinking well of the Serving King will radically impact your feelings toward the King.

But just as important is the recognition of how much God loves you. It is the awareness of God's devotion toward you that sparks a response of 'spontaneous' love toward God. "We love because He first loved us" (1 John 4:19). It is in the recognition of a life given for us that the 'spontaneous' love toward that life emerges.

The challenge, of course, is learning to 'think well' of God, to recognize God's love toward us in the midst of the chaos life often throws at us, for life is rarely neat and clean; to the contrary, it is often messy and unruly. Only those who learn to see the 'love of God' in the midst of the chaos will experience this 'absolute spontaneity' of love toward God. "He who did not spare His own Son but gave Him up for us all..." (Romans 8:32). Intentionally seek to 'see' the love of God in the seeming chaos and discover the 'absolute spontaneity' of love toward God. Those who will sustain the 'trek after God' will do so only after they have discovered the 'absolute spontaneity' of a love toward God.

Day 122

NO GILT-EDGE

...for we walk by faith, not by sight.
(2 Corinthians 5:7)

"...when God begins to use us in His enterprises, we take on a pathetic look and talk of the trials and the difficulties and all the time God is trying to make us do our duty as obscure people. Can we do our duty when God has shut up heaven? Some of us always want to be illuminated saints with golden haloes and the flush of inspiration, and to have the saints of God dealing with us all the time. A gilt-edged saint is no good..."– Oswald Chambers

Often, in those early days trekking after the Serving King, the journey seems to have a 'blessedness', a 'gilt-edge', in which everything comes out 'golden', as the saying goes. At some point, the 'gilt-edge' seems to wear off, and life, with its rough and tumble churning, seems to dull the 'gilt-edge', perhaps even wearing it down to nonexistence. You will be tempted to think God is no longer pleased with you, now that the 'gilt-edge' is gone, the 'flush of inspiration' waning, the 'saints of God dealing with us' less and less of the time. The trek, the adventure of a lifetime in these early stages, becomes a series of 'trials and difficulties' and we 'take on a pathetic look', wondering where the 'gilt-edge' has gone. What happened to the luster? Has God abandoned us?

Thus, the trekker enters a 'season' of walking "by faith, not by sight." This season of walking by faith, and not by sight, can be exceedingly trying at times. It forces the trekker to 'trust God' in the midst of trying circumstances, and that is never easy, never comfortable. But more pressing, more problematic, is the threat of 'obscurity', the horror of not being noticed, not being recognized, toiling away in the shadows of recognition, unnoticed by God or man, or so you think. However, in the solitude of 'obscurity' the 'mettle' of the trekker is manifest. With the 'gilt-edge' gone, God 'knows' the condition of the one being forced to 'walk by faith'.

Anyone can walk the life of the 'gilt-edge'; that "saint is no good" to the purposes of God. But those who shine without the 'gilt-edge', without the 'golden life', without that constant 'illumination of God', those are the saints who shine brightest in the 'enterprises' of God. It is that saint who hears, "Job well done, good and faithful servant!" Trek on in obscurity if need be.

Day 123
THE INDEPENDENT REALITY

For still the vision awaits its appointed time; it hastens to the end – it will not lie. If it seems slow, wait for it.
(Habakkuk 2:3)

"Patience is not indifference; patience conveys the idea of an immensely strong rock withstanding all onslaughts. The vision of God is the source of patience, because it imparts a moral inspiration." – Oswald Chambers

Hearing and seeing the "vision of God" can be immensely problematic for the child of God; especially when that "vision of God" does not come with a time stamp, that exact date when it, the "vision of God," will burst onto the scene as reality. In that moment of yet to be expectation, 'walking by faith, not by sight' becomes a waiting game, anticipating God's calling into being that which God has declared will be.

But patience, "an immensely strong rock withstanding all onslaughts," has no dimension of doubt; rather, it rests on the absolute assurance God has indeed given a preview of what is to be, what must be, what cannot help but be. Therein lies the assurance of the vision, never dependent upon what you should do, but rather, what God will do. Nor does it ebb and flow in response to the actions of others. God's vision is precisely that, the reality God will create, will call into being, independent of the effort of those who trek after God.

It is the 'vision', that "immensely strong rock" that inspires, precisely because it assures the one trekking after the Serving King, of a reality that 'will be', a reality that cannot be thwarted by the ineptness of those trekking after the King, nor even those radically opposed to the King. You will be tempted to forget it is 'God's vision', and will seek to 'help it' become a reality, to help God bring God's vision into reality. But God needs no help, even from those who trek after Him; instead, God simply waits for the 'vision's' appointed time.

So, too, you must wait patiently in the assurance God will do what only God can do. Your best efforts will not hasten 'God's Vision' any closer to reality. Nor will your chaos hinder 'God's Vision'. Simply relax in the privilege of having seen what God intends to do. Then trek on...

Day 124

THE UNEXPECTED COST OF PRAYER

**...praying at all times in the Spirit, with all prayer and supplication.
(Ephesians 6:18)**

*"As we go on in intercession we may find that our obedience
to God is going to cost other people more than we thought.
The danger then is to begin to intercede in sympathy with
those whom God was gradually lifting to a totally different
sphere in answer to our prayers."– Oswald Chambers*

Intercession, the kind of prayer beseeching God to bring about God's
vision for 'others', is a risky endeavor, destined to provoke a dangerous
sympathy regarding those whom God moves toward in response to the
supplications of any child trekking after the Serving King. That unantic-
ipated sympathy for the 'other' arises from the sudden realization God
has begun to intercede for the 'other' in ways that had not been anticipated, painful ways, ways stripping the 'other' down, rendering the 'other'
vulnerable to the presence of God.

However, the trekker will often discover the 'prayer of supplication'
was offered under the assumption God would bring relief, not chaos,
into the life of the other. It is that 'other kind of sphere in answer to our
prayers' unnerving the supplicator, that one who braved the risk of prayer
for the sake of the 'other'.

Thus, before praying for the 'other', first count the cost and determine
whether you are willing to pay the price of watching how God deals with
others. Watching your obedience cause chaos in the lives of 'others' is
never easy; especially when your obedience of prayer has such unexpected consequences for the 'other' you lifted in prayer.

When the trial arrives, will you intercede in sympathy for the other
rather than pray for God to finish God's work of stripping down the 'other',
in order for 'gradually lifting to a totally different sphere' to occur? This
is the hard work of 'prayer and supplication', the difficult process of
serious intercession for the sake of the 'other'. Very few intercessors can
engage in this kind of 'prayer and supplication'. But for those few, what
a marvelous reward when the 'other' finally reaches that 'totally different
sphere'. Dare you pray for the 'other' as you trek after the Serving King?

Day 125
ENTER BY THE BLOOD

Therefore, brothers, since we have confidence to enter the holy places by the blood of Jesus...
(Hebrews 10:22)

"We do not identify ourselves with God's interests in others, we get petulant with God; we are always ready with our own ideas, and intercession becomes the glorification of our own natural sympathies. We have to realize that the identification of Jesus with sin means the radical alteration of all our sympathies. Vicarious intercession means that we deliberately substitute God's interests in others for our natural sympathy with them." – *Oswald Chambers*

Early on, very few trekkers after the Serving King understand the price that has been paid for admittance into the 'holy places'. Like a child who does not understand the monthly mortgage mom and dad have paid for 'their house', many enter the 'holy places' confidently, never considering the price, the 'blood of Jesus', paid to gain entrance into the presence of the Living God. Instead, far too many trekkers boldly and casually enter, never giving thought to the 'price paid' for their right to enter.

But entrance into the 'holy places' was secured by the Great High Priest, who understood that any who would enter the 'holy places' must do so having surrendered all 'interests', but those of God. In the words of the Great High Priest, "Nevertheless, not my will but yours" (Luke 22:42). Thus, the seriousness of entering the 'holy places' is laid bare before us, challenging all trekkers to lay down all 'natural sympathies' to seek only the 'sympathies' of God, the interests of God.

Thus, the radical nature of intercessory prayer, "Seek ye first the Kingdom of God" (Matthew 6:7). There is no room in the life of intercessory prayer for 'natural sympathies', only those 'altered sympathies', the 'sympathies' of God. So the trekker must pause and consider, "Why am I here today? To plead my sympathies or to discover and pledge allegiance to the 'sympathies' of God?" Fear not entering the 'holy places' with yet 'unaltered sympathies'. That is precisely why Jesus paid the price of admission for you. But be prepared, having entered 'by the blood of Jesus' to be altered in ways you could have never anticipated. Those who enter 'by the blood of Jesus' will not leave the 'holy places' unaltered. Be prepared to identify with the interests of the Serving King as you trek on.

133

Day 126

IN AN UNEXPECTED WAY

**For it is time for judgment to begin at the household of God.
(1 Peter 4:17)**

"Every element of self-reliance must be slain by the power of God. Complete weakness and dependence will always be the occasion for the Spirit of God to manifest His power."– Oswald Chambers

For the child trekking after the Serving King, a tendency develops to consider the possibility of 'judgment' in relationship to those deficiencies in our lives. After all, it is those deficiencies that reflect the failures in our attempts to mimic the Serving King. However, the judgment of God comes not in relationship to failures arising out of weakness, to the contrary, grace abounds in and for those moments; instead, judgment thunders into those areas of life in which we have relied on our own 'self-accomplishment' rather than the Spirit of God.

You will be tempted to say, "But I am fully engaged for the glory of God." It is in that moment of 'utter self-reliance' the trekker faces the judgment beginning at the household of God. You have been called to liberation from the condition of self-reliance, the condition of 'every man', and freed for utter dependence upon God and God alone. For it is in those moments of profound weakness, devastating inability, radical shortcomings, that the glory of God shines forth in the most amazing ways.

Indeed this judgment, falling first on the house of God, strips you of all pretense of self-sufficiency, rendering you helpless and utterly dependent on the power of God, manifest so brightly in the midst of your weakness. You will, however, be tempted to resist this judgment that 'crucifies the flesh', knowing that to suffer this kind of judgment is to lose those final precious pieces of your 'independent being' that have hidden themselves in service to the King. But God will find them. In that moment, "it is time for judgment to begin at the household of God."

Now is the time to accept the liberation of judgment, knowing those who have been judged are finally free indeed. Bask in the judgment beginning at the household of God.

Day 127
NEVER YOKE ANOTHER

For freedom Christ has set us free; stand firm therefore, and do not submit again to a yoke of slavery...
(Galatians 5:1)

"Bow your neck to His yoke alone, and to no other yoke whatever; and be careful to see that you never bind a yoke on others that is not placed by Jesus Christ. It takes God a long time to get us out of the way of thinking that unless everyone sees as we do, they must be wrong. That is never God's view. There is only one liberty, the liberty of Jesus at work in our conscience enabling us to do what is right."–Oswald Chambers

It is a dramatic thing for a child trekking after the Serving King when they finally, authentically, begin to hear the voice of God offering opportunities to go 'this way' or 'that way'. For those who hear the voice of God clearly, dramatically, beyond a shadow of a doubt, a horrible temptation arises to place the command of God on the life of those around you, who likewise seek the Living God. You will be tempted to think, "If God desires this or that thing for my life, then surely God will want it for everyone else as well;" thus, the temptation to become God's mailman for the community around you.

Rest assured, the job of 'God's mailman' was filled long ago. The Holy Spirit, the communicating arm of the Godhead, long ago accepted the responsibility to deliver the wisdom and desires of God to each one trekking after the Serving King. But neither are you called to silence. Instead, those trekking with the Serving King are called to 'pick up their yoke' and follow alongside Him, sharing with all who ask, 'the kind of yoke that Jesus has given'.

Beware the greater threat, the temptation to turn away from Jesus to examine the 'yoke' that He has placed on another. If you pause to look, ponder the yoke of another, He will see your transgression, your hesitancy, and indeed you will hear those words Peter heard on that fateful afternoon, "What is that to you? You follow me (John 21:22)!" Never place your 'yoke' on the life of another. Further, never compare 'yokes' with that of another. Understand God loves each one so personally that every 'yoke' is custom-made to lead each trekker to that place God has uniquely created. Pick up your 'yoke', focus on Jesus and trek on.

135

Day 128
HOW MANY TOWERS?

For which of you, desiring to build a tower, does not first sit down and count the cost, whether he has enough to complete it? (Luke 14:28)

"All that we build is going to be inspected by God. Is God going to detect in His searching fire that we have built on the foundation of Jesus some enterprise of our own? These are days of tremendous enterprises, days when we are trying to work for God, and therein is the snare."– Oswald Chambers

We would like to think most of us deciding to trek after the Serving King have carefully counted the cost long before taking that first step; and indeed, we have 'counted' what could be counted. But trekkers soon discover those hidden costs, those yet unaware costs, costs that cannot be known until deep into the journey, when yet unbuilt 'towers' are called for, in lands long away from those of the first 'towers'. It is in that moment the trekker understands there are a good many 'towers' to build and each must be decided upon before launching out toward 'towers' yet ahead.

Therein lies the great temptation for those trekking after the Serving King, to seek contentment in 'towers' already built, 'towers' comfortable and paid for, 'towers' requiring just minor maintenance from time to time. However, the Serving King is never content to 'settle in', instead pressing deeper and deeper into the 'promised land', that land of communion with God, an intimacy rendering the need for 'towers' moot.

In that moment of sudden clarity, the trekker begins to understand these 'towers' we have built are nothing more than "some enterprise of our own" constructed on the "foundation of Jesus." Jesus has merely been the 'stepping stone' upon which we have built 'towers' that must be left behind, for 'towers', by their very nature, can never be taken along on the journey by those trekking after the Serving King. Thus, that moment of startling clarity arrives; 'towers' ought rarely to be built by those trekking after the Serving King. Those who build them run the risk of 'staying with them' as the Serving King continues His journey toward the 'promise land'. "...sit down and count the cost" of the tower you are tempted to build. Don't be startled when He tells you to scrap the project and simply keep trekking on after the Serving King.

Day 129
RECKLESS CONFIDENCE

**Because you have kept My word about patient endurance...
(Rev. 3:10)**

"Patience is more than endurance. A saint's life is in the hands of God like a bow and arrow in the hands of an archer. God is aiming at something the saint cannot see, and He stretches and strains, and every now and again the saint says–'I cannot stand any more.' God does not heed, He goes on stretching till His purpose is in sight, then He lets fly... Faith is not a pathetic sentiment, but robust vigorous confidence built on the fact that God is holy love... Faith is the heroic effort of your life, you fling yourself in reckless confidence on God."– Oswald Chambers

For those trekking after the Serving King, there will be those moments along the trek when you will join with countless others before you in screaming, "My God, my God, why have You forsaken me?" (Matthew 27:46) In those moments of 'patient endurance' you will discover whether or not your 'faith' in God is some 'pathetic sentiment', destined to decay when God and life stretch you to your limits, or whether your 'faith' is your 'vigorous confidence' in God, that 'heroic effort' sustaining you in the midst of the utter chaos and injustice.

You will be tempted to pull back and hesitate in this trek you have been on as you follow the Serving King. You must, in that moment of hesitation, resist the temptation to lose heart and surrender your 'vigorous confidence' in exchange for 'pathetic sentiment'. In this moment of hesitation you must "fling yourself in reckless confidence on God," for it is only in the fire of the trial that the mettle of your confidence in God expresses itself.

Tragically, if your 'faith' does become 'pathetic sentiment', and you shrink back from the trek, you will never discover the "purpose in His sight," as your arrow is retuned to the quill and never released by the archer. Stand firm, "fling yourself in reckless confidence on God." Join Job in proclaiming, "Though He slay me, yet will I trust Him..." (Job 13:15). Recklessly trek on...

Day 130

NEVER CONFUSE VISION WITH DREAMS

Where there is no prophetic vision the people cast off restraint...
(Proverbs 29:18)

"'Where there is no vision ...' When once we lose sight of God, we begin to be reckless, we cast off certain restraints, we cast off praying, we cast off the vision of God in little things, and begin to act on our own initiative." – Oswald Chambers

Dreams and 'prophetic visions' are easily confused. Dreams are the wishful thinking of those trekking after the Serving King. They are mere fantasies dancing in the mind of the beholder, reflecting a make pretend world fluttering this way and that. While dreams comfort and entertain, they have no moral fortitude driving the trekker to 'be and do' what God has called into being. Dreams usher in no new realities; dreams simply provide a momentary smile. Most importantly, dreams are generated by the mind of the trekker, not God.

But 'prophetic visions' are a far different matter. 'Prophetic visions' arise from the very essence of God. They are not simply 'dreams' or wishes emanating from the mind of God; to the contrary, they are 'realities' God promises to bring into being, in space and time. Thus, 'prophetic visions' are rooted in the nature and character of God. They are yet an unseen reality breaking onto the horizon, and the trekker has been given the glorious privilege of previewing that, which, is about to 'be'.

The 'prophetic vision' comes with an unexpected power suddenly and comprehensively, beginning to 'restrain' the 'seer' in ways that could not be anticipated. The trekker suddenly engages in a 'course change' grabbing and constraining the trekker to go 'this way', not 'that way'. The freedom to 'drift off course' is rendered moot. The 'prophetic vision' is so compelling, you can only 'freely' choose to follow the 'prophetic vision' regardless of what it may cost to follow.

And you will wonder, can I throw off this way of 'being and doing' now constraining my life in so many ways, at so many levels? Can I throw off these 'restraints', break free to return to a more comfortable course of my own choosing? Of course. You only need look away, shield your eyes from the vision and join the masses, "cast off restraint." Better yet, simply trek on.

Day 131
MAKE EVERY EFFORT

**For this very reason, make every effort to supplement your faith
with virtue.
(2 Peter 1:15)**

*"We are in danger of forgetting that we cannot do what God
does, and that God will not do what we can do. We cannot
save ourselves nor sanctify ourselves, God does that; but
God will not give us good habits, He will not give us character, He will not make us walk aright. We have to do all that
ourselves..."– Oswald Chambers*

For those trekking after the Serving King, there comes, sooner or later, that moment of frustration when you discover God is not going to do 'this' or 'that' for you; rather, you must "make every effort to 'supplement your faith with virtue." Early in the trek you will find many things requiring 'little effort' to bring about new dimensions of 'virtue' to your life. As the trek continues deeper and deeper into the being of God, you will discover levels of 'virtue' you have never envisioned for yourself, thinking only 'others' would ever reach such 'virtue'. The Spirit of God calls you to go deeper into the 'virtuous' life; and you will be tempted yet again to say, "I cannot do that, it is too hard for me. God must do that for me."

But you are wrong. If you 'cannot' then God would have already done it for you. No, it is not a matter of what you 'cannot' do; rather, a matter of what can only be done by making 'every effort', and that is an exhausting and daunting task. Many will simply settle for what has been obtained already. They are content to watch as 'others' make 'every effort', continuing deeper and deeper into the character of God. Others will make 'some effort', but will fail, falling short of the highest 'virtues' God intends for those who trek after Him. They will proclaim "I tried but could not do it," and that is true, for a partial effort will never achieve those 'virtues' of the highest kind.

Yet, there will be those who 'make every effort' and by doing so discover ways of 'being and doing' far exceeding what could have been imagined previously. They will stand amazed, thrilled, in awe of the power God has endowed as they continued making "every effort to supplement faith with virtue." In that moment of success they will understand the 'power of God' invading the effort of those who make 'every effort'. Trek on with every effort.

Day 132

CULTIVATED LOVE

**...and godliness with brotherly affection, and brotherly affection with love.
(2 Peter 1:7)**

The knowledge that God has loved me to the uttermost, to the end of all my sin and meanness and selfishness and wrong, will send me forth into the world to love in the same way. God's love to me is inexhaustible, and I must love others from the bedrock of God's love to me... Neither natural love nor Divine love will remain unless it is cultivated.–Oswald Chambers

The virtues of a lesser kind, those not requiring 'every effort' (2 Peter 1:5) to thrive, often appear in the life of a child trekking after the Serving King, almost spontaneously. However, 'virtues' of a higher kind, those requiring 'every effort', rarely appear in the life of those trekking after the Serving King; especially this 'virtue' of the rarest kind, that of 'love'. 'Love', at least 'love' in the form of divine love, cannot arise spontaneously out of any heart; rather, it must be carefully 'cultivated', nurtured in such a way that it blossoms spontaneously in the life of the child trekking after the King.

Like all flowers of the Spiritual life, 'love', divine love, cannot be 'cultivated' until it has first been planted; hence, it cannot rise up out of the fleshly nature and character of the one in whom love will appear. No, first, 'love' must be 'poured out in us' (Romans 5:5), prior to any cultivation the trekker must do. You will be tempted to think, "Aha, all I need do is wait for God to 'pour out' His love in me and then I will be able to 'love' as He 'loves'", but that is surely not the case. God has already 'poured out His love' and you must go about the task of making 'every effort' to cultivate that 'love' into an 'inexhaustible' love toward others rising out of the 'bedrock of love' God has poured into you.

It is cultivation of a special kind that will enhance this 'poured in love of God', enabling it to thrive and blossom. First, you must walk closely with God, for 'God's love' thrives in the presence of God. God's presence feeds this 'poured in love' in ways nothing else can. Furthermore, you must choose to see what 'can be', not 'what is', in the life of those you are called to love. 'Love' is drawn toward that which is "good, pleasing and perfect." Allow 'love' to see the very best in those you are called to love. Finally, act decisively in allowing 'love' to express itself. Then, and only then, will you learn the art of 'loving as God loves'. Make every effort to cultivate the 'love that has been poured in'.

Day 133
IS THERE ANY FRUIT?

For if these qualities are yours and are increasing, they keep you from being ineffective or unfruitful in the knowledge of our Lord Jesus Christ.
(2 Peter 1:8)

"The right thing to do with habits is to lose them in the life of the Lord, until every habit is so practiced that there is no conscious habit at all. Our spiritual life continually resolves into introspection because there are some qualities we have not added as yet."– Oswald Chambers

At some point in this trek after the Serving King, you will begin to realize the trek ought to be more than simply a long walk with the King. You will pause to ask, "Is there any 'fruit' from this journey I am on? Is this walk productive for me or for others?" In that moment, you will have hit a key mark in your transformation into a 'Christ Follower' in which pragmatism matters.

Yet, some trekkers will be content in their 'knowledge of our Lord Jesus Christ', but for those who trek closely with the King, there will be no satisfaction in the luxurious life of 'head knowledge' left unapplied for, by definition, 'unapplied knowledge' is 'ineffective and unfruitful'. Instead, these few trekkers will radically examine the 'productivity' of their efforts, and upon finding shortcomings creating a fruitless life will continually engage in 'introspection', looking for "some qualities we have not added yet," some virtues that are yet missing, some way of 'being and doing' that is still absent from day-to-day living. Thus comes the need to ensure these qualities are increasingly yours.

Beware, 'introspection' is fraught with pitfalls for those trekking after the Serving King. Introspection reveals a good number of virtues, 'these qualities', still needing to be added to your repertoire, and it can be overwhelming, unless the trekker remembers God is the source of all 'virtues' yet lacking in the 'being and doing' of the trekker. Your responsibility is simply to 'make every effort' (2 Peter 1:5). It is God Who provides the missing virtues as God endues your 'every effort' with a power beyond what you are able to provide. "For it is God Who works in you, both to will and to work for His good pleasure" (Philippians 2:13). Yours is simply to 'make every effort' as you trek on.

Day 134

CLEAR CONSCIENCE?

**So I always take pains to have a clear conscience
toward both God and man.
(Acts 24:16)**

*"God always educates us down to the scruple. Is my ear so
keen to hear the tiniest whisper of the Spirit that I know what
I should do? "Grieve not the Holy Spirit." He does not come
with a voice like thunder; His voice is so gentle that it is easy
to ignore it. The one thing that keeps the conscience sensitive to Him is the continual habit of being open to God on
the inside."– Oswald Chambers*

The 'pain' of a 'clear conscience' does not come naturally for those trekking after the Serving King. To the contrary, most of us trekking after God, or not, avoid pain whenever possible, which is especially easy once you realize the voice of the Holy Spirit "does not come with a voice like thunder; His voice is so gentle that it is easy to ignore it." Therein lies the problem, the temptation to 'ignore' the Holy Spirit through easy access to 'noise' hindering us from ever hearing that 'painful' whisper as the Spirit speaks to the conscience.

Thus, you will have to "take pains to have a clear conscience toward God and man." First is the 'pain' of decreasing the distracting 'noise' pre-venting you from hearing that small, peaceful voice speaking directly to your conscience. Hence, the 'noise' of the TV, computer, smartphone, etc., will have to be silenced with great intentionality, and silenced long before the fatigue of the day has set in. The Spirit's voice rarely rises above the distraction of competing noise. Second is the 'pain' of lis-tening to the conviction of 'sin'. "And when He comes, He will convict concerning sin and righteousness and judgment" (John 16:8). Only those who have been convicted and cleansed of 'sin' can "have a clear con-science toward God and man."

Then, the final dimension of 'pain', actualizing what the Spirit makes known to the conscience. You will be tempted to delight in 'knowledge', but 'knowledge', the conviction of the Holy Spirit, only becomes 'fruitful' when that 'knowledge' is actualized in the form of your 'being and doing' as the Spirit of the Living God leads. Rest assured, this will not be easy deep into the trek after the Serving King, for the Spirit of God will con-vict "down to the scruple." And you will be amazed at just how small a 'scruple' gains the attention of the Spirit. Trek on...

Day 135
KEEPING FIT

...always carrying in the body the death of Jesus, so that the life of Jesus may also be manifested in our bodies.
(2 Corinthians 4:10)

"You must keep yourself fit to let the life of the Son of God be manifested, and you cannot keep yourself fit if you give way to self-pity. Our circumstances are the means of manifesting how wonderfully perfect and extraordinarily pure the Son of God is. The thing that ought to make the heart beat is a new way of manifesting the Son of God. It is one thing to choose the disagreeable, and another thing to go into the disagreeable by God's engineering. If God puts you there, He is amply sufficient."– Oswald Chambers

For the modern trekker, the idea of being 'fit' is a topic of great conversation as our culture falls deeper and deeper into 'unfitness'. With that unfitness comes a greater and greater dependency on a 'pill for this' and a 'pill for that'. Nonetheless, we are the most educated, unfit people in the world. Ultimately, our bodies, crushed under the burden of 'unfitness' and 'self-pity', render us unable to find our way back to 'fitness', and so we read more on health and fitness and take another pill. "...and you cannot keep yourself fit if you give way to self-pity."

But 'self-pity', the great crippler of those who desire to trek after the Serving King, must be slain, crucified, rendered moot in the life of those who would trek after the King. In its place must manifest the 'life of Jesus' Who has every intention of being 'manifested in our bodies'. Then the 'cultural obsession with fitness' becomes clear. 'Fitness' is an essential part of being able to 'trek' after the King. His is not an 'agreeable' trail, but, rather, often 'disagreeable by God's engineering'; for it is in the 'disagreeable' that we discover the manifestation of, "how wonderfully perfect and extraordinarily pure the Son of God is."

Then the 'aha' moment arrives. 'Fitness' of the flesh, of our physical bodies, is but a precursor of the 'fitness' that really matters, manifesting the image of the Son in our 'being and doing', having learned to 'master the flesh' en route to mastering the spirit of the inner being. "You must keep yourself fit to let the life of the Son of God be manifested." Only then can you trek even deeper into the being and doing of the Son.

Day 136

SAME MISERABLE CROSSPATCH?

...having the eyes of your hearts enlightened, that you may know what is the hope to which He has called you, what are the riches of His glorious inheritance in the saints.

(Ephesians 1:18)

"You cannot do anything for your salvation, but you must do something to manifest it, you must work out what God has worked in. Are you working it out with your tongue, and your brain and your nerves? If you are still the same miserable crosspatch, set on your own way, then it is a lie to say that God has saved and sanctified you."– Oswald Chambers

Many trekking after the Serving King are shocked to discover how little has changed in their essential condition deep into the trek. Some are still the "same miserable crosspatch" that began the trek many days gone by. Grace, because of its adequacy even in our most horrific failures, can make it easy, though not comfortable, to stay in a 'crosspatch' condition (bad-tempered person). Oh, the misery of the 'crosspatch' in Christ.

If the trekker is not careful, that 'crosspatchness' can become an ever-present condition, rendering salvation in the present moment empty of 'his glorious inheritance' that Christ has intended for those who trek after Him. Instead of a 'glorious inheritance' made accessible in the immediacy of the present moment, the 'glorious inheritance', that radiance and transformation into the image of Christ, remains just that, a 'thing' that is yet to come, in a future too far away to be seized and claimed in the present moment. Many, lacking the 'eyes of your enlightenment', will never seize that 'glorious inheritance', never 'enlightened' enough to see it, thinking it only for a time when death and decay has been robbed of their victory.

But this 'glorious inheritance' Christ has made ready for you is already deep within you, vibrant and present, latent in the residing presence and power of the Holy Spirit. This 'glorious inheritance' need only be 'worked out', manifested in the present moment, now that God has carefully 'worked in' this 'glorious inheritance', the living presence of the Spirit of God. The 'glorious inheritance' has been yours all along. When will you let God manifest the glory that is now yours in Christ? 'Work out' what God has 'worked in' and the 'crosspatch' will be no more. Leave the 'crosspatch' behind as you trek on.

Day 137

THE LUXURY OF MISERY

...by which He has granted to us His precious and very great promises, so that through them you may become partakers of the divine nature, having escaped from the corruption that is in the world because of sinful desire.
(2 Peter 1:4)

"And He will tax the last grain of sand and the remotest star to bless us if we will obey Him. What does it matter if external circumstances are hard? Why should they not be! If we give way to self-pity and indulge in the luxury of misery, we banish God's riches from our own lives and hinder others from entering into His provision. No sin is worse than the sin of self-pity, because it obliterates God and puts self-interest upon the throne."– Oswald Chambers

The promise, a 'very great promise', of the inheritance that is ours in Christ ought not to be considered a promise of a life of ease. No such promise is ever offered to the child trekking after the Serving King. Instead, the 'very great promise' is the privilege to "become partakers of the divine nature" as found in the life and example of Jesus the Christ. For those who accept the privilege to embrace the 'inheritance' of the 'divine nature' in the present moment, access to the lessons of the divine nature become available immediately, but in an unexpected form. "Although He was a Son, He learned obedience through what He suffered. And being made perfect..."

But suffering is never easy, even when initiated by 'partaking of the divine nature', as suffering brings with it the great temptation of 'self-pity', that loathsome condition before God rendering the one trekking after God useless. In that moment of self-pity, the purpose of God, that 'making perfect' by what is suffered, is lost in the most tragic way of all; because the suffering that was meant to bring to "perfection through obedience" is rendered purposeless as the trekker wallows in the 'luxury of misery' and 'self-pity'.

There may be no more detestable experience in life, in the trek after God, than to suffer in a purposeless manner. Thus, you must stand tall in the midst of your suffering and rest in the assurance that your 'suffering' is enriched and made valuable by the purpose of God being manifest as you move toward a 'perfection' found in the 'divine nature'. Only by embracing the circumstances God strategically sets into place can you find liberation from the "corruption that is in the world because of sinful desire." Trek on, painful or not.

Day 138

SON OF MAN

**While He blessed them, He parted from them and
was carried up into heaven.
(Luke 24:51)**

*"The Ascension is the consummation of the Transfiguration.
Our Lord does now go back into His primal glory; but He does
not go back simply as Son of God: He goes back to God as
Son of Man as well as Son of God. There is now freedom of
access for anyone straight to the very throne of God by the
Ascension of the Son of Man."– Oswald Chambers*

For the those trekking after the Serving King, the realization that He
has ascended to His 'primal glory', not just as the glorious Son of God,
but equally as the Son of Man, is hopeful news for those who desire
to access not just His 'divine nature' (2 Peter 1:4), but, in addition, His
redeemed 'human nature'. That is the central message of His 'incarnation', the redemption of 'human nature', the reclamation of our way of
'being and doing' and His ascension as the Son of Man is the testament
to the completion of the redemption of the 'human condition'.

Thus, the intent of the 'glorious inheritance' becomes clear. The child
trekking after the Serving King is empowered to follow the reclamation of
'human nature', our way of 'being and doing', and that reclamation was
never intended to be an isolated feat by the one man Jesus, instead, a
reclamation by all those who would seek to do as He has done.

You will be tempted to simply wave goodbye as He is carried "up into
heaven" to sing songs of praise and glory to the ascended Son of Man,
this Redeemer of fallen humanity. Then the startling challenge, "now
freedom of access for anyone straight to the very throne of God." But
you will pause, fearful you have not 'reclaimed' and 'redeemed' enough
of your 'being and doing' to freely follow the Son of Man into the throne
of God. However, it is the journey into the presence of God, into the
presence of 'His primal glory', that the 'inheritance' awaits, empowering
you to return to the 'workshop' of reclamation, the human condition,
where you too must become a 'son of man', here and now, redeemed
and cleansed by the abiding 'primal glory' of God. Then it dawns on you
again, He is leading us yet again toward more than we have dared to
dream or imagine. Trek on...

Day 139

SPONTANEOUS BEING

Look at the birds of the air: they neither sow nor reap nor gather into barns, and yet your heavenly Father feeds them... Consider the lilies of the field, how they grow: they neither toil nor spin...
(Matthew 6:26-28)

"Our heavenly Father knows the circumstances we are in, and if we keep concentrated on Him we will grow spiritually as the lilies." – Oswald Chambers

For those trekking after the Serving King, the challenge to remain focused on the King becomes increasingly difficult as our attention is drawn back over and over again to the mundane, those basic necessities of life. For those seeing only the surface of the teaching of Jesus, rather than the deeper things of "all truth" (John 16:12), the 'truth' lying below the surface of simplicity, the promise of Jesus simply becomes your "Father knows we need them," a simple pledge we will receive those mundane aspects of life: food, clothing and shelter. And, of course, it is that simple.

However, the promise of Jesus is much deeper than the mundane for those who are trekking after the Serving King. Beyond the mundane, Jesus promises a 'naturalness' as a by-product of "seeking first the Kingdom of God and His righteousness" (Matthew 16:33). Indeed, stop and consider the 'lilies of the field'. They neither 'spin' nor 'toil' and yet they 'grow', they become precisely what God has called and designed them to be, simply because that is how God has designed them to function when "seeking after the Kingdom of God."

So it is with the child trekking after the King, "seeking the Kingdom of God and His righteousness." You will neither need to 'toil' nor 'spin' in order to grow. Growth is spontaneous for those "seeking first the Kingdom of God." It is the natural consequence. It simply will happen.

Then, naturally, spontaneously, the child trekking after the King suddenly realizes, "I have no interest in barns. Nor am I anxious about filling a barn." The tyranny of 'worry', that relentless distraction and threat to our uninterrupted trek after the King, simply and naturally falls to the wayside. And the child who has neither 'toiled' nor 'spun' finds a spontaneous freedom from the mundane that enables and enriches the trek in ways never imagined. Trek on toward 'spontaneous being'.

147

Day 140
NOT IMAGINED TROUBLE

Who shall separate us from the love of Christ? Shall tribulation, or distress, or persecution, or famine, or nakedness, or danger, or sword?
(Romans 8:35)

"God does not keep a man immune from trouble; He says – "I will be with him in trouble." It does not matter what actual troubles in the most extreme form get hold of a man's life, not one of them can separate him from his relationship to God. We are "more than conquerors in all these things." Paul is not talking of imaginary things, but of things that are desperately actual."– Oswald Chambers

M. Scott Peck suggested, "To live, is to suffer," and the child trekking after the Serving King expects no exception. Few, however, especially those most faithful to the trek, expect the 'depth' of trouble that awaits. Who could have expected Paul was serious about "tribulation, or distress, or persecution, or famine, nor nakedness, or danger, or sword?" We thought that was a rhetorical question. But it is not. Paul simply reminds the trekker of 'desperately actual' troubles awaiting those who remain engaged in the trek, who risk the trail of obedience.

More debilitating to the trek is the source of some of the more serious trouble. Jesus warned those who would trek deep into the journey with Him, "Indeed, the hour is coming when whoever kills you will think he is offering service to God" (John 16:2). And that is the crippling blow of this 'desperately actual' trouble that no trekker is prepared for. Who can believe it is those fellow trekkers, who likewise are seeking to follow the Serving King that will attempt to deliver a fatal blow to your trek?

You will be tempted, yet again, to abandon the trek, to surrender to the blows of those who seek to end your trek. You will despair, thinking this must be the judgment of God against your trek, that God's love has abandoned you, that you are as vile as those who strike at you declare. But you are wrong. "No, in all these things we are more than conquerors through Him Who loved us...neither death nor life, nor angels nor rulers, nor things present nor things to come, nor powers, nor height nor depth, nor anything else in all creation, will be able to separate us from the love of God in Christ Jesus our Lord" (Romans 8:36). 'These things', these 'desperately actual' things, can never squelch the passion of that child who 'knows' His Lord, who walks with the Serving King, whose hand never leaves the hand of Him who guides in this trek after God. Trek on...

Day 141
A CATNAP OF THE FLESH

By your endurance you will gain your lives.
(Luke 21:19)

"There are certain things we must not pray about– moods, for instance. Moods never go by praying, moods go by kicking... It is a continual effort not to listen to the moods which arise from a physical condition; never submit to them for a second. We have to take ourselves by the scruff of the neck and shake ourselves, and we will find that we can do what we said we could not. The curse with most of us is that we won't. The Christian life is one of incarnate spiritual pluck."– Oswald Chambers

For the child trekking after the Serving King, endurance, especially when you are still yet fresh and spunky in your trek, seems like an unnecessary reminder to be steady in your quest. But endurance has no meaning until you are tired, really tired, exhausted even, ready to surrender to the flesh, to lie down and take ever so brief a nap. It is that spiritual 'catnap', those precious few minutes of surrendering to the flesh, that send you caravanning deep into a slothfulness that robs the spiritual life of its vigor and vitality. And the 'catnap soon becomes a deep sleep.

For those trekkers who succumb to the flesh, even for the moment, a residue clings to the trekker as they attempt to climb back out of the 'catnap', only to discover it is not nearly so easy to arise from the 'catnap' as it is to fall into it, deep into it, so deep you begin to wonder if you should simply rest on, allowing the flesh to have its way?

This battle of endurance is not won after the 'catnap', the ever so short dance with your old ways of 'being and doing'; no, it is won in the moment of the first yawn, that first lure of the 'flesh' to sit down, take an ever so brief reprieve from your trek after Jesus. It is in that first moment that indeed you must "take ourselves by the scruff of the neck and shake ourselves." For indeed, you can shake off the 'flesh' and its whining for a reprieve. You can trek so much farther than you have ever imagined.

Those who endure, who push through the fatigue of trekking after Jesus, will suddenly discover a 'life' that can only be had by those who endure the trek. Of course, once you truly "gain your lives," you will never ever look back toward the old ways of 'being and doing'. In that new life, you will suddenly discover the 'endurance' is over. You have arrived. You have gained a new life. Trek on...

Day 142

LIFE IN THE VILLAGE OF THE KINGDOM

**But seek first the kingdom of God and His righteousness, and all these things will be added to you.
(Matthew 6:33)**

"Jesus is not saying that the man who takes thought for nothing is blessed–that man is a fool. Jesus taught that a disciple has to make his relationship to God the dominating concentration of his life, and to be carefully careless about everything else in comparison to that."–Oswald Chambers

Some who trek after the Serving King will indeed, thinking they are rendering service unto God (John 16:2), become the 'fool', considering nothing but Kingdom building, void of a concern for life in the 'village'. But life is meant to be lived comprehensively, and the 'Kingdom' is meant to break into every dimension of 'village life', those private enclaves where the vast majority of life must be lived. Hence, Kingdom of God seeking does not render 'village life' moot, instead, mandating every aspect of 'village life' be scrutinized under the ethic of Kingdom dwellers, those who seek the Kingdom of God in every aspect of life in the village.

You will be tempted in your trek to think the 'Kingdom' and the 'secular' are meant to be forever separate, much like the folly of thinking separation of 'Church and State' can really happen in some neat and clean process by those who live day to day in the village. But it can't precisely because the Serving King is insistent that those who trek after Him seek the "Kingdom of God and His righteousness" in every dimension of village life, even at City Hall. Of course, you will equally be tempted to insist that others who live in the village also live by the ethics of the Kingdom of the Serving King, but that is not the command of the King; rather, He simply commands those who trek after Him to "seek first the Kingdom of God and His righteousness."

Then the insight arrives. The Serving King lived His entire life radically committed to 'seeking first the Kingdom of God and His righteousness', and did so while in the kingdom of another kind. The Serving King did not mandate how life in the village ought to be lived; instead, He simply invited those who would trek after Him to 'seek' the Kingdom that is yet still arriving. He invites those who trek after Him to 'come and follow me' (Luke 18:22), join in seeking and implementing the 'Kingdom' into every way of 'being and doing'. Watch as the Kingdom rushes in. Trek on...

Day 143

FIEND OR SAINT?

...that they may all be one, just as You, Father, are in Me, and I in You, that they also may be in Us, so that the world may believe that You have sent Me.
(John 17:21)

"God is not concerned about our plans; He does not say— 'Do you want to go through this bereavement; this upset?' He allows these things for His own purpose. The things we are going through are either making us sweeter, better, nobler men and women; or they are making us more captious and fault-finding, more insistent upon our own way. The things that happen either make us fiends, or they make us saints."– Oswald Chambers

Accord and harmony rarely come for those who trek at length together. Even the Serving King, Jesus, found Himself in that awkward moment when His will and the will of His Father seemed to be at odds; and in that moment, that terrifying moment of uncertainty and impending disunity, the 'unity' of the Godhead stood in the balance, threatening the very existence of the Kingdom of God. But Jesus, in that moment of uncertainty, reclines in the 'will' of Him who 'sent me'. "Father, if you are willing, remove this cup from me. Nevertheless, not my will, but yours, be done" (Luke 22:42).

Thus, those who trek after the Serving King ought not to be surprised, or even shocked, when the 'will of the Serving King' stands in stark contrast to that of the one trekking after Jesus. It is the inevitable consequence of following the Serving King into the very heart of God, where even the Serving King discovered a 'will' dissimilar to His own in that precarious moment. In that moment, 'oneness' with the Father, with the Son and with the Spirit teeters on the edge of collapse.

The 'saint' is not the one who agrees with every inclination of the Living God, that will never happen, not even for Jesus; no, the 'saint' is the one who acquiesces to the will of the Living God in spite of their disagreement. But the 'fiend' is that rare trekker who yet knowing, "My ways are not your ways" (Isaiah 55:8) refuses to surrender to the will of God and strikes out in bold allegiance to the 'will of self'. And the greatest 'fiend' of all is that rarest of trekker who 'self-sanctifies' his own will, pretending it to be that of the Serving King. Follow the example of Him Whose will was surrendered to the will of the Father "that the world may believe You have sent Me." Trek on in sweet surrender.

Day 144
INFIDELITY OF A DIFFERENT KIND

Therefore I tell you, do not be anxious about your life, what you will eat or what you will drink, nor about your body, what you will put on. Is not life more than food, and the body more than clothing? ...and all these things will be added to you.
(Matthew 6:25,28)

"Have you ever noticed what Jesus said would choke the word He puts in? The devil? No, the cares of this world. It is the little worries always. I will not trust where I cannot see, that is where infidelity begins. The only cure for infidelity is obedience to the Spirit."– Oswald Chambers

Learning to implement the ethics of the Kingdom into day-to-day life in the 'village' can be cause for 'anxiety' for some who are intent on trekking after the Serving King. You will be tempted to think, "This will work in the Kingdom of God, but it will not work in the 'village' next door to the Kingdom of God." Thus, for those who actually implement Kingdom principles into 'village' life, the temptation to fret will be constantly on the horizon. The words of the Serving King will do little to alleviate your concern, "is not life more than food, and the body more than clothing?"

However, the challenge of the Serving King is simply a warning to those who would trek after Him, a reminder God is ever aware of the genuine needs in life. Yet, it is so very easy to find oneself consumed with a concern for the basics of life, especially when one's primary energy is spent on 'Kingdom building'. It is that 'angst' or 'anxiousness' that distracts, much like the driver who 'texts' while whirling through town. The distraction, the worry about 'what you will drink' or 'what you will put on,' is not the intentional infidelity of adultery; rather, the infidelity of the 'wandering eye' that Jesus warned His followers of. It is not blatant unfaithfulness; instead, it is just the mild distraction diverting attention just long enough to miss an important turn. It is the infidelity of a different kind that will 'choke' the "word He puts in."

This 'choking of distraction' will happen ever so slowly, and you will not realize you have lost sight of the King until it is too late. Beware of this infidelity of another kind. It, too, can do much damage to the trek you are on.

Day 145
THE TOUCH

**When I saw Him, I fell at His feet as though dead.
But He laid His right hand on me, saying, "Fear not."
(Revelation 1:17)**

"Whenever His hand is laid upon you, it is ineffable peace and comfort, the sense that 'underneath are the everlasting arms,' full of sustaining and comfort and strength. When once His touch comes, nothing at all can cast you into fear again."– Oswald Chambers

Few who are trekking after the Serving King expect to actually arrive at their destination, in the very presence of God, in all of His radiance, glory and power; at least not until death has opened the door to His throne room. John, stripped of death's preparation, that precious shedding so critical to bowing in the presence of the King, suddenly finds himself in the very presence of Almighty God, the resurrected Christ, armed and ready for the summation of history, and, not surprisingly, merely falls prostrate, 'as though dead', at the feet of Jesus. A fear so comprehensive, even for this man 'touched' by the 'Word made flesh' so many times before, that even breath itself ceases for the moment.

In the presence of the Christ, all of His presence, the full glory and power that is truly His, stripped of all the humility of incarnation, all pretense of our comfortableness falls by the wayside. There is no posture but the 'appearance of death' at His feet. Fear, like a fear you have never known, will indeed radiate in every fiber of your being. It cannot be avoided. It is that moment, a horrible moment of uncertainty, even after the many days of trekking with and after Him, that each of us will wait for that touch of 'sustaining comfort and strength', and in that touch find the ability to stand in the presence of the reigning God and King.

No child trekking after Jesus can be prepared for that moment of full exposure to the glory and radiance of the King of Kings stripped of the humility of incarnation. Like John, you, too, will fall 'as though dead', prostrate at the feet of Jesus, and wait in that incredibly quick, long moment for His touch. It is a touch that heals and liberates, removing all fear of the Glorious King. Indeed, you will never know fear again, ever again; instead, you will gracefully trek after the Serving King as one who has survived 'the touch'.

Day 146

THE FREEDOM TO GO LEFT OR RIGHT

"Is not the whole land before you? Separate yourself from me. If you take the left hand, then I will go to the right, or if you take the right hand, then I will go to the left."
(Genesis 13:9)

"Whenever right is made the guidance in the life, it will blunt the spiritual insight. The great enemy of the life of faith in God is not sin, but the good which is not good enough. The good is always the enemy of the best."– Oswald Chambers

Deep into the trek after the Serving King you will begin to discover a 'freedom' to go left or right at many of the crossroads coming your way. What a glorious moment in the journey as you begin to realize the 'wrong turns' were left behind long ago in your trek. Now all trails lead to the Serving King. All roads are His paths.

Abraham has reached that glorious moment in his life where he understands it does not matter which direction he goes or which land he takes. The land itself is completely irrelevant to the blessing that awaits him. His blessing lies not in the 'promised land', but rather in the God Who blesses and anoints the land which has been promised. Hence, he can boldly announce to Lot, "You choose, left or right, it matters not to me." Abraham has arrived at the 'promised land', that wonderful realization circumstances and land have no value in and of themselves; rather, it is the presence of God that ensures the 'promised land'.

Thus, Abraham chooses what is 'best', to trust God for His blessing rather than the land itself. He is free to choose what is best, to trust God, not landscape. Rest assured when your left or right matters, God will make it known to you, ever so clear to you. But those who are genuinely seeking after the Serving King ought not be surprised when all paths lead to the King. Left or right matters not. God will anoint and bless either path you take. Indeed, the 'good' is to ask God, "Which direction should I go?" But oh the joy of being deep enough into the trek, into His ways of 'being and doing', that left or right no longer matters. Seize the 'best', the utter confidence that left or right matters not. All that matters is trusting God to create the 'promised land', desert or oasis. Delight in the bliss of knowing you have chosen the 'best', trusting God in all conditions. Trek on in the confidence you are so deep into the quest that 'left or right' no longer matters...

Day 147
PRAYER OF A DIFFERENT KIND

Rejoice always, pray without ceasing, give thanks in all circumstances; for this is the will of God in Christ Jesus for you.
(1 Thessalonians 5:16-18)

We think rightly or wrongly about prayer according to the conception we have in our minds of prayer. If we think of prayer as the breath in our lungs and the blood from our hearts, we think rightly. The blood flows ceaselessly, and breathing continues ceaselessly; we are not conscious of it, but it is always going on...Prayer is not an exercise, it is the life. – Oswald Chambers

Paul's words seem foreign to many trekking after the Serving King. Of course, they seem foreign because we have wrongly conceptualized prayer as an activity of words, rather than a way of 'being and doing'. But this 'being and doing', this life of prayer, does not come prewired into our being like "blood flows ceaselessly, and breathing continues ceaselessly"; no, it is a learned way of 'being and doing' that must be engrained into our being in such a way that it occurs spontaneously, effortlessly. That engraining cannot happen overnight. It is a learned way of 'being and doing'.

At some point, however, the child trekking after the Serving King begins to understand 'all circumstances' are part of the 'will of God'. It is that understanding that opens the door for a new way of 'being and doing', recognizing the hand of God at work in all of life's circumstances, even the very worst life throws our way. It is in that moment of recognition that the child of the King begins to understand the power of God is at work in all circumstances, that we have been invited to influence the manner in which God 'works' in the particulars of each and every moment.

Then, the opportunity to 'rejoice always' appears in that moment of comprehension, understanding God is always at work, life is void of meaningless accidents. Prayer becomes that act of 'engagement' in which the child of the Serving King seizes the moment to act out the purpose of God in the messy particulars of the moment. Prayer unleashes 'being and doing' into the messy particulars of God's unfolding purpose. To live, to 'be and do', is to pray, to engage in the 'purpose of God' as it unfolds in the moment. For the child trekking after the King to live is to 'pray without ceasing'. Trek on in prayer.

Day 148

WAIT

"...I am sending the promise of my Father upon you. But stay in the city until you are clothed with power from on high."
(Luke 24:49)

"The parenthesis in John 7:39 ("For the Holy Ghost was not yet given; because that Jesus was not yet glorified") does not apply to us; the Holy Ghost has been given, the Lord is glorified; the waiting depends not on God's providence, but on our fitness."– Oswald Chambers

Those words of Jesus must have been incredibly difficult to hear for those disciples so intent on trekking after the Serving King. The Risen Lord, Whom they have faithfully followed, appears ready to give marching orders to those who have most trusted Him and are finally ready for battle. The command of the King finally arrives, "Stand down." Thus begins a long 50 day wait for the "power from on high."

You will be tempted along the way to engage in the work of the Serving King in your own strength and wisdom, and this temptation will intensify as you see more and more of what the Kingdom of God is really all about, as you begin to understand what needs to be done, how 'being and doing' should look in the life of a follower of the King. The temptation will come when you begin to think, "I can do that," and off you will run into 'being and doing' as the Serving King desires; but simple or not, easy or not, you will not be able to sustain a life of 'being and doing' over the long haul. Therein lies the problem. A lifetime of 'being and doing' is an incredibly long trek necessitating power of a special kind.

Stamina is the key for those whose life of 'being and doing' lasts over the decades, over the many miles that have to be trekked, the ever-changing conditions of terrain requiring a lifetime of creativity in your 'being and doing'. This kind of stamina can only be found in the abiding presence and empowering of the Holy Spirit. So Jesus calls those who would follow Him to 'wait', ever so patiently, for the "power from on high," essential to sustaining the trekker over a lifetime of 'being and doing'. For those who wait, 'fitness' falls into our being as the power of the Holy Spirit flows into every moment of 'being and doing'. This trek is a long one. Wait until you have received the "power from on high."

Day 149
PERSPECTIVE IS EVERYTHING

In that day you will ask nothing of Me.
(John 16:23)

"Until the resurrection life of Jesus is manifested in you, you want to ask this and that; then after a while you find all questions gone, you do not seem to have any left to ask. You have come to the place of entire reliance on the resurrection life of Jesus which brings you into perfect contact with the purpose of God."– Oswald Chambers

Perspective is everything in a life spent trekking after the Serving King. Early on, the trek is filled with uncertainties, questions and doubts about so many aspects of the trek. However, as time passes, the Holy Spirit provides deeper and deeper insights into the character of God, the ways of God, the very being of God, and so the questions begin to ebb, slowly but surely, as understanding becomes ever so clear in 'this or that' particular.

But be warned, increased understanding will never settle all the 'open ends' and uncertainties of your trek. No, you were never meant to follow because you understand the particulars of God's purposes, how each detail interlocks with all the other details of God's plan, or the outcomes of this or that action. Instead, you are simply meant to "trust in the Lord with all your heart, and do not lean on your own understanding" (Proverbs 3:5). And 'trust' is indeed something you can do in the midst of great uncertainty. Of course, Jesus was speaking of that day in Glory, when the dull mirror becomes clear, and you see all that can be seen, all that can be known, and the questions stop, literally stop, now knowing what can be known.

But, what of today? Or, perhaps tomorrow? Can a child trekking after the Serving King reach that "place of entire reliance on the resurrected life of Jesus which brings you into perfect contact with the purpose of God?" Indeed, many trekkers before you have found that place of peace and contentment in the 'present moment'. It is found not in knowing the particulars of this or that, but rather in the utter confidence "for it is God Who works in you, both to will and to work for His good pleasure" (Philippians 2:13). You cannot 'manufacture' such utter confidence in God; rather, it is a fruit of the Spirit of God dwelling deep within you. In the meantime, 'trust' until that 'utter confidence' is yours. Trek on in the midst of your questions.

Day 150
WHEN IS 'THAT DAY'?

"In that day you will ask in My name, and I do not say to you that I will ask the Father on your behalf; for the Father Himself loves you, because you have loved Me and have believed that I came from God."
(John 16:26-27)

"Our Lord does not mean that life will be free from external perplexities but that just as He knew the Father's heart and mind, so by the baptism of the Holy Ghost He can lift us into the heavenly places where He can reveal the counsels of God to us."– Oswald Chambers

One day, more precisely, 'that day', the child trekking after the Serving King will begin to sense a radical shift in the relationship with the God the Father. The Serving King will intentionally, by design, begin to withdraw from the 'mediation role' that He has provided you as you related to the Father. And as the Mediator withdraws, the 'Father's promise', "and behold, I am sending the promise of My Father upon you" (Luke 24:49), begins to meld your relationship to the Father, in the same fashion as the Serving King experienced through the 'empowering of the Holy Spirit'. It is in that 'oneness' through the Spirit that lines of communication, direct communication, begin to flow into the Father-child relationship. Thus, Jesus startles us by saying, "I do not say to you that I will ask the Father on your behalf." It simply is not necessary. The Father loves you.

But, when? When is 'that day', the day in which the Father loves so directly that the child's questions need no Mediator? It is the day in which you begin to hear, better yet, 'understand' the whispers of the Holy Spirit, those impulses to 'be and do' in 'this or that' particular way of 'being and doing'. It is the day in which the Spirit does indeed begin to "teach you all things and bring to your remembrance all that I have said to you" (John 14:26). It is 'that day' in which your question begins with, "Father..."; rather than "Jesus..."

In 'that day' you will have discovered a new depth of relationship with the Father, a relationship that is direct and more personal than your relationship with God has ever been. You will suddenly discover that your trek, intent upon following the Serving King, is now often hand in hand with the Father. Trek on...

Day 151
COMMON SENSE PITFALLS

**Yet another said, "I will follow You, Lord,
but let me first say farewell to those at my home."
(Luke 9:61)**

"'Yes, I will obey God if He will let me use my common sense, but don't ask me to take a step in the dark.' Jesus Christ demands of the man who trusts Him the same reckless sporting spirit that the natural man exhibits."– Oswald Chambers

At some point, early for some and late for others, Jesus will demand of you obedience that flies in the face of 'common sense', that way of 'being and doing' culturally trained and deployed by those 'common' members of a 'common' community. Often, that demand to abandon 'common sense' seems to come in the midst of the most inconsequential requests or demands of Jesus, "let me first say farewell." Thus, you will be tempted to ignore the command of Jesus, thinking 'this issue' to be not only 'uncommon in sense', but inconsequential as well. Could Jesus really deny a quick visit to say goodbye?

However, it is not the 'farewell' itself creating the problem; rather, it is the nature of the Serving King to continue moving forward, creating a great distance between those who would 'look back' and the ever forward-moving King. Playing 'catch-up' is oh so difficult in this trek after the Serving King. Thus, the warning from Jesus concerning those who 'look back' as not 'fit' for the Kingdom of God.

Never confuse what 'Jesus might have commanded' with what 'Jesus did command'. The former leaves much room for 'farewells' and a host of other activities. But the latter, clarity regarding what Jesus did say, ought never be delayed, regardless of how inconsequential or 'uncommon sense' things appear. You will have to decide, in the most radical way, to simply obey Jesus when 'clarity' is present. Those who delay simply are not fit, and will not 'catch-up' to the forward-moving Christ. Engage that 'reckless sporting spirit' in the most profound manner possible and trust the Serving King to provide appropriate 'farewells' whenever and wherever needed. It is in that moment of 'reckless sporting spirit' that the best 'farewells' unfold. Trek on while the Serving King bids those around you a 'farewell' fit for a reckless servant of the King.

Day 152

THE OPTIMISM OF TRUST

But Jesus on His part did not entrust Himself to them, because He knew all people and needed no one to bear witness about man, for He Himself knew what was in man.
(John 2:24-25)

"Our Lord trusted no man; yet He was never suspicious, never bitter, never in despair about any man because He put God first in trust; He trusted absolutely in what God's grace could do for any man." – Oswald Chambers

Crowds often gather trekking after the Serving King, many of whom will be as radically committed to following the Serving King as you are. That should be your first hesitation in considering whom you will trust as you journey along after the Serving King. Those walking beside you are just like you, frail and broken.

Some, knowing who the 'others' are, understanding their likeness, will surrender to cynicism, despairing of 'all men', knowing them to be all damaged by the 'slavery of sin' (Romans 7:14). Others, knowing not even their own degraded being, will foolishly trust others who are trekking after the King. Neither option is adequate for a lifetime of 'divine optimism'.

Instead, there is the way of Jesus, whose optimism toward those trekking behind was rooted in an absolute trust in God, whose grace abounds in every moment of the trek. That grace does not mandate that all those trekking after the Serving King measure up to expectation; rather, it is a pledge to those who must have a 'divine optimism of trust' concerning 'others' from time to time, that God is always at work, in every moment and circumstance bringing about God's purposes in the midst of an 'optimism of trust'.

You will be tempted when others fail to measure up to expectation, either the expectation of Jesus, or worse yet, your expectation, to cast them off, to declare them 'untrue' in their quest after the Serving King. But then, you remember, they are just like you. And then the joy of the 'optimism of trust', the attitude of Jesus, rekindles your spirit, and you reach to assist up that one who has failed, as together you trek on.

Day 153
THE UNBEARABLE POSSIBILITY

**And He said to me, "Son of man, can these bones live?"
(Ezekiel 37:3)**

*"When God wants to show you what human nature is like apart
from Himself, He has to show it to you in yourself. If the Spirit
of God has given you a vision of what you are apart from the
grace of God (and He only does it when His Spirit is at work),
you know there is no criminal who is half so bad in actuality
as you know yourself to be in possibility."– Oswald Chambers*

Deep into the trek after the Serving King, a depth that only time and relationship to the Serving King can provide, will be that moment in which the trekker 'looks back' and sees, really sees, just how far they have come in this quest after the Serving King. The changes, the actual transformation, will be stunning, profound, even breathtaking, for those who have journeyed deep into the quest. But there is a 'dark side' to this transformation, hidden deep within the experience of transformation, a 'forgetfulness' of just how far this trek has been, just how much 'trans-formation' God really has brought about. In that 'forgetfulness' you will be tempted to think you have always been this way, or, at least, were close to 'being this' early on in the journey.

You are wrong, of course. The grace of God has done more than you could have ever dared to dream or imagine. Grace has renewed you, it has rebuilt you, it has 'graced you' with a 'forgetfulness' concerning what you once were. In that forgetfulness you stumble upon the 'other', the 'old bones' of the 'other', scorched and so profoundly entrenched in the slavery of sin, and the Serving King asks you, "Can these bones yet live?"

Then, the flash of memory, the full recollection of the 'old bones, scorched beyond recognition, that had once been you, "the Spirit of God has given you a vision of what you were apart from the grace of God." And you remember the "unbearable possibility" of what you could have been, what you once were apart from the grace of God. Having been touched by God's grace, you remember 'any old bones' can live, for you are the living testimony of that glorious reality of 'old bones' alive and full of vigor and life. Oh, how grateful you are that the "unbearable possibility" is indeed dead and buried as you trek on in the redemption of Him Who gives life to 'old bones'.

Day 154

THAT FIRST FEARFUL STEP WHO IS THE MAN WHO FEARS THE LORD?

**Him will He instruct in the way that he should choose.
(Psalm 25:12)**

"We rob ourselves of the marvelous revelation of this abiding companionship of God. 'God is our Refuge'– nothing can come through that shelter."– Oswald Chambers

The 'fear of God' appears from time to time for the child trekking after the Serving King. It comes in those unsettling moments of insight into the nature and being of God, when our cozy and comfortable images of God are replaced with terrifying insights into the 'actual, incomprehensible understanding' of Who and What God is. Until you have 'seen' it, understood it in that 'clouded' manner, you cannot imagine that 'knowing' God would produce such fear.

This 'fear' from understanding, of genuinely comprehending the nature and being of God, is a doorway every trekker must walk through. Most will not walk through it early in the trek, but rather, delay until deep into the quest, when such fear can be harnessed and made useful. The Psalmist wrote, "The fear of the Lord is the beginning of wisdom; all those who practice it have a good understanding" (Psalm 111:10). However, this 'fear' of comprehension will be overbearing if you are not pre-warned, prepared for this overpowering 'fear' that has stricken so many before you.

This 'fear' is indeed the 'beginning of wisdom', for it is only in genuinely understanding the nature and being of God that you will have opportunity to understand the why of God's ways, to embrace the simple reality God's ways are not your ways. Then comes the difficult moments of the trek after the Serving King, those moments of 'practice' in which the ways of God are 'put into play, demonstrating a 'good understanding' of the ways of God. Yes, in the moments following comprehension of God and His ways comes the inevitable fruit of fear, the urge to say, "I am too afraid to 'be and do' what God has shown me to 'be and do'. I am immobilized, stricken by a fear that hinders me from 'good understanding.'"

Then, the glorious remembrance of the first days of the trek, 'one step at time' surfaces. Indeed, the journey of a thousand miles begins with that fearful first step. Trek on...

Day 155
DELIGHTING IN JOY

The friendship of the Lord is for those who fear Him...
(Psalm 25:14)

"What is the sign of a friend? That he tells you secret sorrows? No, that he tells you secret joys. Many will confide to you their secret sorrows, but the last mark of intimacy is to confide secret joys."– Oswald Chambers

Those trekking after the Serving King often find their relationship with Him oriented around 'need'; thus, the early conversations are one-dimensional, 'need-oriented' ones in which God is often used as a mere resource for life, producing friendship of the most shallow and common form. But for those who continue the trek, contentment does come, a contentment rooted in relationship rather than the acquisition of 'favors'. In that contentment a change of conversation begins to unfold.

However, the real test of friendship is not simply your willingness to share 'secret joys', critical as that may be, but, more importantly, the response of the one with whom you share this last vestige of friendship. Therein lies the secret of intimacy with God, knowing that God is delighting in your every success, your every joy. Oh, the blessing of hearing God's joy concerning your successes in life. In that moment you have discovered the first vestiges of genuine friendship.

Then comes the critical moment. God shares God's joy with you, that way of 'being and doing' that brings joy to the heart of God. You discover God's delight in blessing those whom God loves. More importantly, God's greatest joy is watching you mimic God's way of 'being and doing', blessing and enriching the lives of others, sometimes at great personal expense. Oh, the joy of a life well spent.

Suddenly, the trek becomes a walk amongst two friends, a friendship so rich and deep that each knows the other to be a safe haven to confide those 'secret joys'. A relationship in which two kindred spirits become one, one in spirit, one in 'being and doing', one in relating to the world. Such a friendship is rare for both the child trekking after the Serving King, and the King Who serves. You are on the cusp of such intimacy. Trek on...

Day 156
THIS IS THE NEW NORMAL

"I will never leave you nor forsake you."
(Hebrews 13:5)

"Sometimes it is not difficulty that makes me think God will forsake me, but drudgery. There is no Hill Difficulty to climb, no vision given, nothing wonderful or beautiful, just the commonplace day in and day out– can I hear God's say-so in these things?"– Oswald Chambers

Deep into the trek after the Serving King, another simple truth begins to appear on the horizon concerning the nature of the 'trek' itself. Early on, the trek is filled with great mountains to be conquered, challenging 'crossings' of 'this kind or that', difficult life changes mandating utter reliance on God in each present moment. The early days of transformation are profound and challenging.

Then, quite unexpectedly, the trek flattens out, the scorching challenges of transformation are completed, and a startling 'mundaneness' settles into your trek. Your magnificent quest evolves into a simple walk with the Serving King. There is peace in the land, and your walk, your 'being and doing', settles into normalcy, a normalcy quite different from the 'old normal', as the 'new normal' settles into place.

In that 'new normal', this new way of 'being and doing', you will begin to wonder if the Serving King still walks by your side, still values your presence, now that life has settled into the 'new normal', a new way of 'being and doing' seeming to require so little, if any, 'divine assistance' to carry on? You will pause and wonder, why would the Serving King stay so close to me in this 'new normal' of mundaneness in everyday life?

However, in the 'new normal' dependency upon the Serving King in the 'present moment' has become part of your being, part of your 'everydayness' of life. It is not that life has indeed become so easy, but rather, you have finally learned to lean on His Spirit in each and every moment of the "commonplace day in and day out." He has finally become the 'foundation' for your commonplaceness. And that, of course, changes everything.

It is in this commonplaceness that 'oneness' with God has finally arrived. Rest assured that the Serving King has not moved on toward those who need Him more; rather, utter dependency upon Him in each moment has become the 'new normal'. Know that the shaded flatlands will not last forever. There are still mountains to be conquered in your quest. Trek on in the commonplace. The mountains will come soon enough.

Day 157
THE REALITY OF OBSTACLES

...for He has said, "I will never leave you nor forsake you." So we can confidently say, "The Lord is my helper; I will not fear; what can man do to me?"
(Hebrews 13:5-6)

"Are you learning to say things after listening to God, or are you saying things and trying to make God's word fit in? Get hold of the Father's say-so, and then say with good courage–"I will not fear." It does not matter what evil or wrong may be in the way, He has said–"I will never leave thee."– Oswald Chambers

The obstacles within the trek are real and no child trekking after the Serving King should lose sight of that reality. Some obstacles are intended for your path, others for the path of another, and the key, of course, is to know which obstacles are for you and which are meant for the 'other'. The key to staying on course, 'your course', is "learning to say things after listening to God." It is only after listening to God that one ought to boldly say, "That obstacle is meant for me and I shall go the way God has asked."

Some will foolishly engage every obstacle appearing on the horizon, assuming all possible obstacles are meant to be 'your obstacles'. But not every possible obstacle is meant for you; rather, you have forgotten many others are trekking after the Serving King and the paths of the many crisscross often throughout a lifetime. So you must learn to 'hear Him' concerning the many possible obstacles before you. When in doubt, 'stand down' until you are sure the obstacle ahead is meant for you.

But rest assured, should you mistakingly stumble upon an obstacle intended for another, the Serving King will not abandon you; instead, "we can confidently say, 'The Lord is my helper, I will not fear!'" For indeed, "It does not matter what evil or wrong may be in the way, He has said, 'I will not leave thee.'" Thus, there is no obstacle in life you will face alone, regardless of the 'wrong' path you may be on, and you will occasionally be on those 'wrong paths'. God is your companion and will journey with you on both the 'right' or 'wrong' path. More importantly, God will not only journey with you on the 'wrong' path, but will speak to you yet again on how to return to the 'right' path. Fear not. Trek on with Him Who continues to guide on all paths.

Day 158

THE RESTORED WILL

**...work out your own salvation with fear and trembling.
(Philippians 2:12)**

"The profound thing in man is his will, not sin. Will is the essential element in God's creation of man: sin is a perverse disposition which entered into man."– Oswald Chambers

You began your trek after the Serving King under great duress. Such is the simple reality for all trekkers, crippled by a 'will' enslaved to sin. Yet, the 'will' remembers what it was designed to do in trekking after the Serving King and so begins the battle for mastery of the 'will'. Sin is no easy opponent, fighting for mastery of the 'will' in each moment, finding victory in far too many battles along the way. Although, many liberated by the prevenient empowering grace of God, choose to 'trek after' the Serving King.

Immediately upon taking the first step of this great trek, God continued a 'good work' in you, a restoration of the 'will' liberating from sin, the will's old taskmaster, and freeing it to 'do' what the 'will' was always meant to do: please God. Once engaged on the trek after God, God responds toward the 'will', "for it is God Who works in you, both to will and to work for His good pleasure" (Philippians 2:13). As you quickly discover, God does not intend to work alone. No, God has liberated the 'will' to work with God, alongside God, in this 'restoration' of not only 'will', but additionally the 'life' of the one who has been redeemed.

However, this 'work out' requires great effort on the part of the 'liberated will' and it must engage a 'flesh' that has been infected in the most profound manner by 'sin', that nagging inhibitor, the great detractor of all movements toward the 'divine'. Therein lies the great first effort for the 'liberated will', the seduction of the flesh, returning it toward its original calling: pleasing God. Be not surprised as a persistent 'fear and trembling' lingers in your being. You have engaged in this battle many times before and lost, as the 'flesh', infected and empowered by 'sin', reigned over your 'will', rendering you a slave to its desires. But things have changed in the most profound manner, for God is now at work within you, empowering the 'will' in ways never before imagined. The victory is now yours. All that remains is to simply 'work it out' in the midst of the 'fear and trembling'. Trek on...

Day 159
AN UNEXPECTED FRUIT OF KNOWING

"Whatever you ask in My name, this I will do, that the Father may be glorified in the Son".
(John 14:13)

"Am I fulfilling this ministry of the interior? There is no snare, or any danger of infatuation or pride in intercession, it is a hidden ministry that brings forth fruit whereby the Father is glorified. Am I allowing my spiritual life to be frittered away..."– Oswald Chambers

Knowing the Serving King is the most essential aspect of the life of intercession. Without 'knowing', so much of what is asked for is void of 'His name', thus impotent and 'frittered away' as all 'unknowing' must be. Hence, the caution of Jesus to first, "ask in My name." However, this 'in His name" does not come to those who occasionally dwell in His presence; but rather, to those who have learned to 'abide in Me' (John 15:4), and that 'abiding' does not come quickly. It is reserved for those who trek ever so closely to the Serving King.

When this 'knowing' finally comes into being, that certainty of 'your will' being 'His will', intercession takes on a 'power' only possible when endued with the enabling of the Christ, the Serving King, Who unleashes His power in ways beyond what we could have imagined. Suddenly, intercession takes on a potential far beyond the prayer of uncertainty, that pleading with God precisely because you do not 'know' what 'His will' would mandate. It is the 'knowing' of 'abiding in Him' that ushers in a new way of unleashing the power of the Serving King.

Yet 'knowing' is never enough: it is but the precondition for 'this I will do'. It is the simple act of 'asking' that unleashes the power of the Serving King. So you must ask with great determination, 'knowing' that you are in the 'right', aligned in the will of the Serving King. Be not surprised when He does what He has promised to do, 'this I will do'. It is the 'unexpected fruit' of knowing. Those who 'know' discover a way of 'being and doing', interceding, ushering in new realties that change every aspect of life for those blessed by your intercession. Bless those around you with the 'unexpected fruit of knowing' the One Whom you trek after.

167

Day 160
OBEDIENCE IN THE MUNDANE

**"If you know these things, blessed are you if you do them."
(John 13:17)**

"It is a great deal better to fulfill the purpose of God in your life by discerning His will than to perform great acts of self-sacrifice. "To obey is better than sacrifice." Beware of harking back to what you were once when God wants you to be something you have never been."– Oswald Chambers

The mundaneness of trekking after the Serving King can become disheartening for those longing for the 'high praise' of "great acts of self-sacrifice." Self-sacrifice is not difficult to manufacture in a life surrounded by those so very willing to allow you to do so on their behalf. But self-sacrifice is never, by simple definition, obedience unto to God. Only sacrifice called for by God has any value; hence, a critical first step is 'to know these things' before engaging in any great task for the Kingdom of God; especially the task of 'self-sacrifice'.

Being prepared for that rare, yes very rare, 'knowing' that calls for self-sacrifice is important, but that is not the 'norm' for a child trekking after the Serving King. The norm, rather than calling for 'great sacrifice', is the simple challenge to ignore the 'great sacrifice', and in its place, shocking as it may seem, the mundane call to simply obey in day-to-day business of life. Samuel voiced the mundane challenge, "Behold, to obey is better than sacrifice, and to listen than the fat of rams" (1 Samuel 15:22).

When the rare call to 'self-sacrifice' does not come, be prepared for the common, the mundane, clarity of direction regarding the less glorious tasks of everyday living. The simplicity of the mundane will startle you. "Say thank-you." "Pray for her." "Buy his lunch." "Pray for this meal." "Forgive." And countless others. None of the mundane tasks of obedience will qualify under the guidelines of 'self-sacrifice' in and of themselves; but, make no mistake, there is a cumulative effect upon the life of 'immediate obedience' in the mundane.

There in the midst of 'immediate obedience' in the mundane, you discover this "something you have never been." No longer are you stymied by the simplicity of obedience in the mundane looking for just the right 'self-sacrifice'; instead, you have discovered the sacrifice of immediate obedience in the everyday, ordinary moments of life. You have discovered 'obedience in the mundane'. And life, mundane living, will never be the same. Trek on...

Day 161

THE POVERTY OF ABUNDANCE

"For everyone who asks receives, and the one who seeks finds..."
(Luke 11:10)

"'For every one that asketh receiveth.' This does not mean you will not get if you do not ask (cf. Mat. 5:45), but until you get to the point of asking you won't receive from God."– Oswald Chambers

For the child trekking after the Serving King, the 'poverty of abundance' creates an awkward independence from God. The return to 'poverty', that state in which abundance has been surrendered, is difficult to re-create by those who have much. Such was the sad state of the rich young ruler who discovered, simply because he asked, a profound truth revealing his 'poverty of abundance'. Matthew provides the story, "The young man said to Him, 'All these I have kept. What do I still lack?' Jesus said to him, 'If you would be perfect, go, sell what you possess and give to the poor, and you will have treasure in heaven; and come, follow Me'. When the young man heard this he went away sorrowful, for he had great possessions" (Matthew 19:20-22).

It is not an easy thing to discover you have a 'poverty of abundance', the accumulation of many resources keeping you from utter dependence upon God. Harder still is the realization many resources can be acquired apart from God, independent from a relationship with God, unintentionally creating a barrier to intimacy and utter dependence upon God. And you will not "receive from God" until the barriers, those resources acquired independent of God, have been surrendered, laid down, enabling the trek after the Serving King to continue. Therein lies the rub, the hindrance in the journey, for few will brave the question, "Lord, what do I lack?" That is the dangerous question few are willing to consider.

Out of the 'poverty of abundance' come few questions. It is a poverty that robs the spirit of the necessity of seeking God, depending on God, asking God. Without 'asking', 'seeking', there can be no finding of that which only God can provide. Now that you have journeyed with Serving King along this trek, ask Him the question few dare to ask, "Lord, what do I still lack?" Be prepared to lay down much of what you have dragged along the trek thus far. You, too, can be free of the 'poverty of abundance', if you are willing to simply ask. Once laid down, oh how the trek after the Serving King changes. Trek on with your lighter load.

Day 162
NEED OF A DIFFERENT KIND

"...ask, and it will be given to you; seek, and you will find..."
(Luke 11:9)

"Get to work, narrow your interests to this one. Have you ever sought God with your whole heart, or have you only given a languid cry to Him after a twinge of moral neuralgia? Seek, concentrate, and you will find."– Oswald Chambers

Any child trekking after the Serving King will experience those occasional twinges of moral neuralgia, those ever so brief twinges of sharp pain, traveling quickly up the moral spine, reminding the child of the ever-present need to exercise life in right relationship to God. It is not unusual in those moments to reach out toward God, ever so briefly, looking for relief from that pang of moral neuralgia. But never confuse that brief glance toward God with the kind of 'seeking' that 'finds God' in a transformative manner in the present circumstance.

There is another kind of 'seeking' and finding that provides access to God in ways moral neuralgia never can. It is that moment in which 'seeking' God is rooted in a different kind of 'asking', an 'asking' that does not arise out of what you believe you need for life and sustenance, but rather, 'asking' God what He has determined you 'need'. The promise of Jesus to those trekking after Him is so simple and yet profound, "and you will find."

Be not dismayed when God's 'need' list is extensively different from your own, when what you really 'need' is precisely the circumstances in which you now find yourself. It is in that moment of sudden 'need' recognition that life takes on new meaning and new opportunity. What you 'need' is to maximize the opportunities of 'this moment' to unlock fresh new 'needs' for the next moment. What you 'need' is available in the present moment. "Seek, and you will find."

Then the flash of insight comes. The right question arrives. You ask, "Lord, why do I need what You have given me in this particular moment? What am I to learn from what I 'need' right now?" It is 'seeking' within the present circumstances that your 'needs' become clear, that God can be found in the richest manner, that life thrives with meaning and transformation. 'Seize the day', it has all that you 'need'. "Seek, and you will find." Trek on in the assurance of today's needs.

Day 163
IMBUED WITH VITALITY

**"Come to Me, all who labor and are heavy laden,
and I will give you rest."
(Matthew 11:28)**

*"'and I will give you rest,' i.e., I will stay you. Not–I will put
you to bed and hold your hand and sing you to sleep; but–I
will get you out of bed, out of the languor and exhaustion,
out of the state of being half dead while you are alive; I will
imbue you with the spirit of life, and you will be stayed by
the perfection of vital activity."– Oswald Chambers*

Fatigue for the child trekking after the Serving King is seldom the
by-product of being 'poured out' (Philippians 2:17) by too much activity;
rather, it points to a disturbing lack of relationship with the One Who
imbues with power and vitality. But you will be tempted to say from time
to time, "I have nothing left to give. I am worn out." Indeed, what 'you'
have to give will have been 'poured out' and exhaustion, that profound
fatigue rendering you limp, unfit for use in the Kingdom of God, will cause
you to wilt under even the slightest service unto the King. The trek will
end, as you lay exhausted by the wayside.

Thus will come the proclamation, "I am 'burned out', unable to carry
on, and a sabbatical of rest is needed. Thus, I am going to hide and rest
until my strength has been restored." The temptation to 'step out' of the
trek after the Serving King will clamor for your attention. But rest, the
cessation of 'serving the King', will do little to restore your strength, for it
is not the 'work' that has exhausted you; rather, it is the lack of intimate
fellowship with the Christ. Jesus is very clear, "My burden is light." His
burden will never fatigue you.

Understand that the cessation of 'activity', service rendered unto the
King, will do nothing to restore the 'strength' that matters, that imbuing
of power and vitality flowing forth from communion with the King. The
illusion of restored vitality following that period of 'rest' will last only for
the moment, only until what 'you' have to give has been quickly vanquished yet again. If you are not careful, pausing to understand what is
happening, this cycle of fatigue and rest generates a repeating pattern
plaguing you for a lifetime. Instead, 'abide in Him' and discover "the
perfection of vital activity." Join those who trek with the endless energy
imbued to those who have learned to 'know Him'. Trek on...

Day 164
ACTUALITIES OF LIFE

He said to them, "Come and you will see." So they came and saw where He was staying, and they stayed with Him that day, for it was about the tenth hour.
(John 1:39)

"'They abode with Him that day.' That is about all some of us ever do, then we wake up to actualities, self-interest arises and the abiding is passed."– Oswald Chambers

Anyone, even the mere novice, can abide with the Serving King for a day, a mere 24 hours of focused attention. That kind of trek, the brief encounter, is attractive to a vast number of would-be followers of Jesus who prefer the safety of encounters with Jesus 'late in the day', in the 'tenth hour', and away from the 'actualities' of day-to-day living. But the key to a lifetime of trekking after the Serving King is to learn to string together a great number of days without interruption, a honeymoon of sorts. It is the issue of 'interruption' that creates the dilemma for many who would trek after the Serving King. Life is full of interruptions and the 'honeymoon', uninterrupted days with the Serving King, simply come to an end. It cannot be avoided, the 'actualities' of life will return; hence, a new strategy must be found if you are to 'stay with Him' for a great number of days.

Therein lies the 'secret' to sustaining the trek, day after day, for indeed you will "wake up to actualities," those ever-present, meddlesome realities of life, beckoning you to return from your siesta with Jesus. Now you must say to Jesus, "Come and you will see." The 'secret' is not to be found in abiding with Jesus for the day, but rather, inviting Him to 'Come and you will see" the 'actualities' of your life, how your life unfolds in the 'actualities' of each and every day.

By inviting Him into your 'actualities', you will discover the wonderful reality that Jesus had planned to 'come and you will see' all along. He intends to walk with you, at your invitation, examining all the 'actualities' of your life. He has no intention of simply 'saving' you from the 'actualities' of your life; no, it is His intention to redeem those 'actualities', to imbue them with life and vitality, to make your 'actualities' vehicles of redemption and grace. But He waits for your invitation to 'come and see'. Trek on by inviting the Serving King to 'come and see' the 'actualities' of your life.

Day 165

FISHING IN THE PERFECT STORM

**And Jesus said to them, "Follow Me, and I will make
you become fishers of men."
(Mark 1:17)**

*"In the life of a saint there is this amazing wellspring of original
life all the time; the Spirit of God is a well of water springing
up, perennially fresh. The saint realizes that it is God Who
engineers circumstances, consequently there is no whine,
but a reckless abandon to Jesus."– Oswald Chambers*

The 'actualities' of life, those circumstances of the present moment randomly appearing out of the chaos of life, are the direct by-product of the 'engineering God' Who creates precise circumstances in which your 'follow Me' must take place. You will be tempted in your 'following Him' to ignore the 'actualities' of your circumstances, attributing those 'actualities' to 'random chaos', conditions resulting from 'something', 'anything', but the hand of God, rendering this 'present moment' void of meaning and purpose, destined to be merely endured until calmer 'fishing' conditions appear. However, every 'present moment' has been precisely 'engineered', ushering in 'perennially fresh' moments for the Spirit of God.

Jesus is very clear about the intention of the 'engineered random chaos' that God has orchestrated in your ever-present moment. Your random 'actualities', engineered with the precision of the 'master engineer', arising out of the chaos, are nothing more, nothing less, than the creation of the 'perfect storm' in which the 'fishing of men' can best take place. And your false assumption, 'fishing cannot take place in these actualities' in this 'perfect storm', falls by the wayside; replaced with the reality that 'fishing in the storm' of your 'actualities' is precisely what God has intentioned all along. This is the 'perfect storm'.

In that 'perfect storm' you will be tempted to 'whine', "I cannot fish in seas like this!" Of course not. Only Jesus can enable you to 'fish' in these present circumstances, in the 'perfect storm' you are now in. That is precisely what He promised, "I will make you fishers of men". And the flash of insight arrives yet again, 'fishing for men' rarely occurs in calm waters; instead, it is the 'perfect storm' that prepares both the fisherman and the fish. So Jesus said to Peter, "Come. So Peter got out of the boat..." (Matthew 14:29)

173

Mornings With Oswald

Day 168
ABIDING WITH HIM IN THE PUBLIC SQUARE

**"Abide in Me, and I in you. As the branch cannot bear fruit by itself, unless it abides in the vine, neither can you, unless you abide in Me."
(John 15:4)**

"It does not matter what my circumstances are, I can be as sure of abiding in Jesus in them as in a prayer meeting. I have not to change and arrange my circumstances myself. With Our Lord the inner abiding was unsullied; He was at home with God wherever His body was placed."– Oswald Chambers

At some point in the trek, the child trekking after the Serving King begins to understand a profound change in relationship, a change in which 'abiding in Him' transforms from retreating from the 'present actualities' of life in order to 'abide in Him' in the comfort of the 'prayer meeting', to understanding He is 'with you', even in the actualities of the present moment. This understanding changes the nature of the trek in the most profound manner. The need to retreat from 'life' in order to 'abide in Him' slowly begins to recede into the background, a vestige of a former way of 'being and doing' that rendered you absent from so many of life's key moments.

However, to 'abide' with Him in the present actualities, you will have to learn to 'be and do' just as He 'is and does', for you will not sense His "unsullied inner abiding," if you are still trying to 'be and do' in those ways predating His presence, His residence in your inner being. The Christ will not sanctify those ways of being and doing foreign to Him, nor will He pretend to support you in the midst of 'being and doing' violating His way of 'being and doing'. He will not abandon you in those moments of the 'old ways', nor will you sense His 'unsullied inner abiding'.

If you are to "abide in Me and I in you," then you will have to make that difficult decision to be "at home with God wherever His body was placed." Therein lies the battle, understanding the 'location' and 'setting' of your body, in all of its awkward placements in life, sullied as they may be, is always a moment to be 'at home with God'. Make that decision to 'abide with Him' by taking Jesus with you into each and every place your 'body is placed'. Abide with Him in the public square. Stand with Him in the public square. Recognize He has chosen to trek with you into each and every 'present moment'. Together with Him, you can 'be and do' in ways you have not known possible. Trek on...

174

Day 167

THE ORDINARY LIFE

**For this very reason, make every effort to
supplement your faith with...
(2 Peter 1:5)**

"No man is born either naturally or supernaturally with character; he has to make character. Nor are we born with habits; we have to form habits on the basis of the new life God has put into us. We are not meant to be illuminated versions, but the common stuff of ordinary life exhibiting the marvel of the grace of God. Drudgery is the touchstone of character."– Oswald Chambers

No child trekking after the Serving King is thrilled with the proclamation, "Drudgery is the touchstone of character." Nor will the realization that the 'supplements of your faith', "virtue, and virtue with knowledge, and knowledge with self-control, and self-control with steadfastness, and steadfastness with godliness, and godliness with brotherly affection, and brotherly affection with love," can only be added to your being as you "... make every effort" (2 Peter 2:5). Few, especially early in the trek, have the fortitude and discipline to engage in the 'drudgery' of character building.

In a culture of 'immediacy' and 'have it your way', the prospects of character building occurring naturally or spontaneously are not good. The good news is that character building does not occur outside the confines of normative living; to the contrary, almost all character building unfolds in the "common stuff of ordinary life exhibiting the marvel of the grace of God." But therein lies the 'hitch'; the 'common stuff' must be imbued with the 'grace of God'.

However, you will be tempted to continue in the 'previous ways' of engaging the 'common stuff' of life, evading the challenge to 'make every effort' to infuse the 'ordinary' with the very unordinary grace of God. That is the challenge of the trek after the Serving King, learning to elevate the 'ordinary' by the infusion of the grace of God, creating character in your own being by redeeming the drudgery of the ordinary through the infusion of 'grace'. It is the creation of 'habits in the ordinary' that will usher in the elusive 'character of being' so desperately sought by those trekking after the Serving King. Examine your 'ordinary', infuse it with the 'grace of God', and 'marvel' at the 'character' that takes shape in you. Character is the fruit of the ordinary, lifelong trek after the Serving King. Trek on...

Day 168

THE EVOLUTION OF A FRIEND

"Greater love has no one than this, that someone lay down his life for his friends. You are My friends if you do what I command you. No longer do I call you servants, for the servant does not know what his master is doing; but I have called you friends."
(John 15:13-15)

"Jesus does not ask me to die for Him, but to lay down my life for Him... It is far easier to die than to lay down the life day in and day out with the sense of the high calling."– Oswald Chambers

It is the longevity of the trek after the Serving King that threatens the vitality of the trek. Were it a sprint, even a marathon, that would be far easier, but it is not; no, it is a lifetime. The trek is nothing more, nothing less, than a day-by-day walking after the King. It is those endless days, filled with 'laying down life', in the drudgery of the mundane, the ordinary matters of existence, that ultimately threaten to zap the tenacity of even the most well-intentioned trekker. "It is far easier to die."

Jesus understands the necessary nature of relationship required for a lifetime of 'laying down life' as you trek after the Serving King. The 'servant of Christ', that wise soul surrendered to the Lordship of Christ, must evolve in the most profound manner into the 'friend of Christ'. And that is no easy transformation. It, too, occurs one step at a time.

Therein lies the secret to a lifelong journey with Christ. It must be accomplished one day at a time. 'Friendship', the fruit of the day-after-day trek with Jesus, cannot be forced, nor rushed, nor manufactured. It simply happens. You will know when the 'friendship' has taken root. The 'laying down life' will have become a two-way street. And in rushes that moment of 'serendipity', that flush of unexpected joy, the realization you and He have become friends, for you now 'know what the Master is doing'. You get it. You finally see the 'why' of this day-to-day drudgery in the mundane of 'laying down life'. Then you hear it, those cherished words from the Serving King, "I have called you friend."

You cannot force this friendship, nor make it happen. It is found only by those who 'trek on' long enough to experience the 'evolution of a friend'. Trek on for friendship is just around the corner.

Day 169
THE SHEATHED SWORD

"Judge not, that you be not judged."
(Matthew 7:1)

"There is no getting away from the penetration of Jesus. If I see the mote in your eye, it means I have a beam in my own. Every wrong thing that I see in you, God locates in me. Every time I judge, I condemn myself (see Romans 2:17–20). Stop having a measuring rod for other people. There is always one fact more in every man's case about which we know nothing."– Oswald Chambers

The problem with the 'measuring rod', and it is a major drawback to every 'measuring rod', is its reflective mirroring affect for those foolish enough to use one; and you will be tempted to use a measuring rod, rest assured. 'Judging', for better and worse, is innate to the human condition, and the infusion of 'grace' into the human condition strikes at the root of this divine attribute gone horribly wrong through the infection of sin and the consequent distortions to human nature, even within the child trekking after the Serving King. The Divine response to this 'infection' is not to 'improve' or 'heal' this bent in the human condition, but rather to 'ban' the exercise of judgment altogether, "Judge not."

However, the 'judging mechanism', deeply rooted in the human condition, is difficult to reign in, to 'holster' and to render dormant. Thus, Jesus warns those unable to subdue the 'addiction to judge', with its persistent clamoring to be released from the subconscious cell to which the Spirit has banned it, that upon its release it will not fulfill its promise to 'condemn' only those worthy of its wrath; but rather, will do what it has always done, ultimately judging the one who released it from its imprisonment. So, Jesus warns those tempted to release the beast, to stand down, for upon 'judgment's release' what it will search out is not the 'mote in the eye of the other', but instead, the "beam in my own."

'Judgment' will whisper continually in your ear, "I am here to help, to merely point out that which needs to be fixed in both the 'other', as well as thine own eye." But you must resist the 'common sense' pleas of 'judgment'. It has no intention of fixing what it sees. No, 'judgment' is a dangerous sword, wielded to wound and maim all who fall under its watchful eye. Only God dare unsheathe this sword.

Listen carefully to the words of your friend, "Judge not." Every child must carry this sword, but none should fall prey to its use. Trek on with this sword sheathed at all times. This sword cares not who it slays.

Day 170

UNFORTUNATE SEEING

He said, "Come." So Peter got out of the boat and walked on the water and came to Jesus. But when he saw the wind, he was afraid, and beginning to sink he cried out, 'Lord, save me.'"
(Matthew 14:29-30)

"The wind was actually boisterous, the waves were actually high, but Peter did not see them at first. He did not reckon with them, he simply recognized his Lord, and stepped out in recognition of Him and walked on the water. Then he began to reckon with the actual things, and down he went instantly."– Oswald Chambers

Peter's momentary exception to the rule, his trek after the Serving King, even onto the surface of the water, a feat of amazing stature in and of itself, is short lived. Any critique of his trek ought to begin with his stunning exception to the rule, "the man walked on water!" Yet, his exception to the rule soon falters to an even more consistent rule, "Fear kills faith," even for 'water walkers'.

Thus, even the spectacular 'rule breakers' are susceptible to the invasion of 'fear', even when in the very presence of Jesus. This is no small matter. Peter's failure in the midst of the spectacular, occurred just strides away from Jesus. His 'common sense', chained while in the boat, breaks free, empowered by the sight of the wind and the waves. Once free, 'common sense' beckons for its trusted companion, 'fear', a more powerful foe of 'faith' than 'common sense' could ever be. Peter, in this moment, was no match for 'common sense' and 'fear', and 'sinking' became his fate.

But even in great failure, which often follows great success, a lesson every trekker seems to learn at one point or another, almost as if it, too, is a rule, Peter cries out to the One who rescues every successful failure. His Rescuer questions Peter in His gentle way, "Why did you doubt" (Matthew 14:31)? Undoubtedly, Peter must have responded, "Because I saw..."

This is a common pattern for those who trek after the Serving King, especially for those courageous few who continue to jump out of the boat trekking across the water after the Serving King. Get accustomed to sinking every now and then. But never let that stop you from jumping out of the boat, "When Simon Peter heard that it was the Lord, he put on his outer garment, for he was stripped for work, and threw himself into the sea" (John 21:7). Brush yourself off and jump out again.

Day 171
TENDING HIS SHEEP

"Simon, son of John, do you love Me?" He said to him, "Yes, Lord; you know that I love You." He said to him, "Tend My sheep." (John 21:16)

"Jesus did not say—Make converts to your way of thinking, but look after My sheep, see that they get nourished in the knowledge of Me."—Oswald Chambers

Jesus, the Master Shepherd, was not particularly successful in 'tending sheep', if success is measured by the response of the sheep. In fact, a close examination suggests the pre-resurrected Jesus was the victim of a mass 'sheep mutiny', even His own disciples, the 'sheep' of His inner pen, staying clear of Him in the final hours of His shepherding efforts. Hence, for the child trekking after the Serving King there is little surprise in the fact the 'sheep' will require much 'tending' in the days that are to come. Hence, the repeated challenge of Jesus to 'tend My sheep'.

Rest assured, the sheep of Jesus have not changed much since He left. Tending them, especially in regard to making sure "they get nourished in the knowledge of Me," will never be as simple as putting them out to pasture in the presence of the Church or His Word. They will not consume the 'knowledge of Me' as readily as you might hope. Thus, Jesus repeated the question toward Peter, "Do you love Me," for it is the 'love of Jesus' that will sustain you in your 'tending' of His sheep, rather than a motivating love of the 'sheep'.

You will be tempted to think, "If they were like me, thinking like I do, acting like I do, then I would find it much easier to love them, to tend them." Thus, you will set off to make converts to your way of 'thinking, being and doing', teaching them your understanding of how this 'trek after the Serving King' should look. But alas, you will have forgotten a critical dimension of your trek after the Serving King; it is precisely that, your trek, custom built for you by the Serving King. Your trek cannot be the trek of another, nor should it be.

But you can continually create opportunity for His sheep to find the pasture of His Word, for it is His Word offering sheep the opportunity of nourishment. No shepherd can force the sheep to eat, but he can ensure his sheep always have access to nourishment. "Feed My sheep." Trek on...

Day 172

THE BOUNTY OF INTERCESSORY PRAYER

**And the Lord restored the fortunes of Job,
when he had prayed for his friends.
(Job 42:10)**

"If you are not getting the hundredfold more, not getting insight into God's word, then start praying for your friends, enter into the ministry of the interior... Wherever God puts you in circumstances, pray immediately, pray that His Atonement may be realized in other lives as it has been in yours. Pray for your friends now; pray for those with whom you come in contact now."– Oswald Chambers

Those who have 'failed greatly' in their trek after the Serving King, and, yes, we all 'fail greatly' from time to time, often find great compassion for others who likewise have 'failed greatly' in the trek after God. Job was such a man. His failure, common to us all, was a lack of understanding concerning the utterly, devastating chaos of his life, a chaos robbing him of everything in life, a chaos rooted in something other than a lack of righteousness in his own life. Lacking understanding, he failed in the grandest manner by challenging God to demonstrate the 'why' of the blatant chaos. "Oh, that I had one to hear me! Here is my signature! Let the Almighty answer me" (Job 31:35)! And the answer of God thundered down.

His fair-weather friends, a kind of friend common to all people, abandoned him in his moment of need, crushed as he was by the 'unfair' circumstances of life. In that moment of utter failure, his complete lack of trust in the righteousness of God, Job is offered redemption, a redemption resting on the grace of forgiveness toward others, a willingness to extend concern for others, even when all had been lost to the most cruel of unfair circumstances.

In that moment, rising out his utter failure, Job reflects on the 'righteousness' God attributed to him, long before the chaos unfolded, "a blameless and upright man" (Job 1:8). Job forgives and prays for his friends and the bounty of heaven flows down. It is the bounty of intercessory prayer, that rare jewel for those who in the midst of 'unreasonable utter chaos', prayer for the needs of the others. Learn to pray the prayer of intercession as you trek after the Serving King in the midst of your own unexplainable chaos. And be not surprised when understanding flows your way. Trek on...

Day 173
INTERNAL GRUBBING

But you are a chosen race, a royal priesthood, a holy nation, a people for His own possession, that you may proclaim the excellencies of Him who called you out of darkness into His marvelous light.
(1 Peter 2:9)

"The continual grubbing on the inside to see whether we are what we ought to be, generates a self-centered, morbid type of Christianity, not the robust, simple life of the child of God. Until we get into a right relationship to God, it is a case of hanging on by the skin of our teeth..."– Oswald Chambers

The temptation for the child trekking after the Serving King, grafted into the 'holy nation', part of 'a chosen race', is the propensity toward 'self-examination in an attempt to understand and become 'worthy' of the status obtained, that 'royal priesthood' so few seem to find. The desire to 'become', in and of itself, may be an appropriate response from those whom God has so called. But 'self-examination' is a risky endeavor, initiating a dance with 'twin partners', both of whom have no place in the life of 'grace'.

The 'continual grubbing on the inside' in that relentless and unobtainable pursuit of 'worthiness' before God, soon "generates a self-centered, morbid type of Christianity" robbing the child of God of their standing before God, a standing rooted in God's grace, independent of personal achievement. No amount of 'grubbing', even successful transformational 'grubbing', can produce the 'standard of being' rendered one worthy of the 'royal priesthood'. Exhaustion is the inevitable end of this journey into 'internal grubbing' and self-transformation.

Of course, equally detrimental in this 'internal grubbing' is the despair of hopelessness, soon to follow the inevitable recognition that no amount of 'internal grubbing' and consequent effort will produce the 'being' necessary to fulfill divine expectation. Thus, a lethargic effort, or no effort at all, often accompanies those who finally understand the unreachable heights to which God calls. Stagnation soon follows.

However, there is yet another option. Simply accept and rest in the status you have been granted. It was never earned, never can be. Instead, it is the grace of God, the invitation to simply 'be at rest' in the 'holy nation', an honored guest by invitation only.

Day 174

THE DIVINE MIRROR

"For with the judgment you pronounce you will be judged, and with the measure you use it will be measured to you." (Matthew 7:2)

"If you have been shrewd in finding out the defects in others, remember that will be exactly the measure given to you. Life serves back in the coin you pay."– Oswald Chambers

It is the ironic blind spot in the human condition, a seemingly fatal flaw in all of us, enabling and giving life to our temptation to judge, in spite of the command of Jesus to never do so (Matthew 7:1). This temptation comes precisely because we are so inept at seeing the 'cause of judgment' in our own lives, those nagging insecurities demanding the minimization of others. Thus, it is that 'blind spot', far larger than we could have imagined, this inability to see in ourselves what is so clear to us in the lives of others. The 'blind spot' produces a foolish confidence to press on with pronouncing the shortfalls and defects of another. It is the ultimate folly.

Some, even those trekking closely with the Serving King, having heard the warning of Jesus, will be tempted to risk the 'judgment of another', thinking their own lives to be free of that which they see so clearly in the other. Believing the 'other' to be so radiantly guilty and worthy of judgment, thinking Jesus would surely desire this 'want' in the other to be brought into the light of day, they will trod into the realm meant only for God. And it is a realm God shares with no human being.

But be warned no one enters this realm of God untouched, nor returns untarnished from their walk in the land of judgment, the exclusive domain of God. Each child of the Serving King returns with a new 'measure' by which they will be judged. In judging 'another', they have simply lengthened and sharpened the 'measuring rod' by which they shall be measured.

Should you be 'shrewd' enough to see the "defects in others," rest assured what you have really discovered are those amazingly difficult-to-find 'blind spots' in your own life. You have stumbled upon the 'divine mirror'. Wise is the person who sees that 'divine mirror' through every 'defect' spotted in the life of another. That person has discovered an alarming and healing window into their own soul. Trek carefully with the 'mirror' that judges not.

Day 175
THE VITALITY OF GRIEF

He was despised and rejected by men; a Man of sorrows, and acquainted with grief...
(Isaiah 53:3)

"We take a rational view of life and say that a man by controlling his instincts, and by educating himself, can produce a life which will slowly evolve into the life of God. But as we go on, we find the presence of something which we have not taken into consideration, viz., sin, and it upsets all our calculations. Sin has made the basis of things wild and not rational."– Oswald Chambers

Optimism, that endearing and early companion of the child trekking after the Serving King, thrives early in the trek, when the battles and consequent victories in the 'shallow' places of sin are frequent and effortless. However, eventually, the skirmishes fought in the shallow places of sin give way to the deeper stains of 'sin', entrenched in the 'heart and soul', in the very fibers of our being, stubbornly resistant to every effort to root out sin in all of its venues. And no amount of 'rationalization' can change the reality of the tenacity and 'wildness' of sin.

Grief slowly creeps into the life of the child trekking after the Serving King, but not the grief of utter failure; no, there have been far too many victories for that. This grief comes to those desperate to mimic the Serving King, emerging only because of a lack of a comprehensive victory over sin, desperately longed for by those striving to be what only the Christ can be. No, this grief will not ebb. It is the constant companion of the child desperate to be all that He has called you to be.

But be not dismayed, nor even sorrowful, for this grief is a sign of spiritual vitality, present only in those whom the Spirit of Christ is radically at work. You have discovered His grief, the grief of 'incarnation, the grief of the being in a fallen world. But His grief is not the grief of failure or skirmishes lost; rather, it is the grief of 'incarnation', of radical identification with those whose grief He carries, "Surely He has borne our griefs and carried our sorrows" (Isaiah 53:4). Because He grieves for you, carrying your grief and failure, you need not fret over your own grief. It is your grief boldly proclaiming spiritual 'life' and 'vitality' in the child trekking after the Serving King. Grieve on and fret not.

Day 176
THE HOUR OF POWER

"When I was with you day after day in the temple, you did not lay hands on Me. But this is your hour, and the power of darkness."
(Luke 22:53)

"Have you made allowance for this hour and the power of darkness, or do you take a recognition of yourself that misses out sin? In your bodily relationships and friendships do you reconcile yourself to the fact of sin? If not, you will be caught round the next corner and you will compromise with it. If you reconcile yourself to the fact of sin, you will realize the danger at once..."– Oswald Chambers

Sin, the constant lurking companion of the child trekking after the Serving King, is ever opportunistic, biding time, waiting for that 'hour' when the 'power of darkness' might reign, even if for only the moment. Yes, the 'chief priests, elders and officers of the temple' fell prey to this 'hour of darkness'. Nor is sin anxious over its ultimate demise, its lack of lasting success; instead, it is content to inflict superficial wounds upon any and all, especially those who would trek after the Serving King. Even the people of God can fall prey to sin's invasive power.

Be prepared for that 'hour of power' in which sin and darkness gain the upper hand, for ever so brief a moment, an isolated 'hour of power', rendering the child trekking after God, wretched, drenched in failure, pleading Paul's confession, "For I do not understand my own actions. For I do not do what I want, but I do the very thing I hate. So now it is no longer I who do it, but sin that dwells within me" (Romans 7:15-17). It is the 'allowance for this hour', which seems to come sooner or later for each of us that prepares you for this excruciatingly horrible moment, a wretched moment of immense failure, if unprepared for will 'compromise' you, extending the 'hour' into days on end.

Understand the 'hour of power' need not be the exceedingly bad and ugly for the child trekking after the Serving King to fall into that 'wretched' state. The deeper into the trek one is, the more sensitive the trekker to failure. You will be amazed at how easy it is to feel 'wretched' once you "realize the danger at once." Keep a constant vigil for this 'hour of power'. It is part of the trek. But it is never the last word. Trek on...

Day 177
SUFFERING WITH PURPOSE

"Now is My soul troubled. And what shall I say? 'Father, save Me from this hour'? But for this purpose I have come to this hour." (John 12:27)

"Sorrow burns up a great amount of shallowness, but it does not always make a man better. Suffering either gives me my self or it destroys my self. You cannot receive your self in success, you lose your head; you cannot receive your self in monotony, you grouse. The way to find your self is in the fires of sorrow."– Oswald Chambers

Trekking after the Serving King is rarely, if ever, a sorrowless affair. You will be tempted to sidestep sorrow, whenever possible, thinking this cannot be the right track, cannot be God's intention for me. Or, more tragically, you will attribute your suffering to 'sin' in your life, a punishment or by-product of shortcomings in your spiritual journey, and, indeed, there are moments when that may be the case, but those moments are easily spotted and repentance a path soon followed.

But the example of the Christ gives no right of way and leaves no room for 'purposeless' suffering. That kind of suffering would crush any child trekking after the 'Suffering Servant' (Isaiah 53). The key for any Christ follower, especially when heading into the inevitable suffering that enables you to "find yourself in the fires of sorrow," is to stand tall with Jesus in affirming, "But for this purpose I have come to this hour." Understand, that will not mean you can 'see the purpose' in the immediacy of the firestorm; rather, it suggests you believe there is profound purpose in any firestorm God allows, or even causes, to burn toward your path. Never confuse clarity of the 'specific purpose', or lack thereof, with the absolute certainty there is purpose.

It is the certainty of 'this purpose', the purpose of God, enabling you to thrive in the midst of the suffering and trials inevitably coming your way if you follow closely after the 'Suffering Servant'. As the saying goes, "To live is to suffer and those who survive are those who find purpose in the suffering." When you see suffering in the path ahead as you trek after the 'Suffering Servant', utter His prayer often, "But for this purpose I have come to this hour." You will be amazed at the life and vitality flowing your way, as you trust the purposes of God to find fruition in the midst of your 'fires of sorrow'. Trek on across the hot coals of suffering, praying as you walk, "But for this purpose I have come to this hour."

185

Day 178
ACTUALIZED POTENTIALITY

Working together with Him, then, we appeal to you not to receive the grace of God in vain.
(2 Corinthians 6:1)

"Let circumstances bring you where they will, keep drawing on the grace of God in every conceivable condition you may be in. One of the greatest proofs that you are drawing on the grace of God is that you can be humiliated without manifesting the slightest trace of anything but His grace."– Oswald Chambers

Sooner or later, every child trekking after the Serving King begins to recognize a descending amount of control over the circumstances encountered along the trek. The illusion of control, and, yes, it is an illusion for those young enough to still bask in the fantasy of control, fades with each passing season. With the death of the illusion, a profound understanding begins to take shape, ushering in an ever-increasing understanding that God is at work in each and every circumstance, creating the opportunities for the grace of God to transform those touched by it, those wise enough to 'work together with Him' in bringing forth fruit worthy of the 'grace' you have been provided.

'Working together with Him' is not mandatory for the child trekking after the King. To the contrary, 'grace' is often squandered in the void of 'unactualized potentiality'. Power and ability, 'graced' to you by the presence of the Holy Spirit, left unused, dormant, inert, a mere latent potentiality, brings about little or no transformation in the life of the child trekking after the Serving King. But every child who simply 'receives' the 'grace of God' has the potential to do more than they have dared to dream. Nonetheless, this 'grace' must be 'unleashed' and deployed by those who have received such a glorious gift.

Yes, this power is an enabling power that must be actualized by those who have received it. You will indeed sense that you are 'working together with Him' exerting great amounts of energy to accomplish the high calling God has placed upon your life. But sweat you must. This will not come easy, even when empowered by 'grace'. So expect a 'work out' when actualizing the grace of God. God will provide all that is beyond your ability, but God will expect you to 'work with God' in those areas that are well within your abilities. Of course, there is a huge bonus for those who 'work with Him'. All things are possible with God. Trek on into the impossible.

Day 179
THE MYTH OF JUSTICE

**"Do not be afraid of them, for I am with you to deliver you",
declares the Lord.
(Jeremiah 1:8)**

*"Jesus says, in effect, 'Do not be bothered with whether you
are being justly dealt with or not.' To look for justice is a sign
of deflection from devotion to Him. Never look for justice in
this world, but never cease to give it. If we look for justice,
we will begin to grouse and to indulge in the discontent of
self-pity–'Why should I be treated like this?' If we are devoted
to Jesus Christ we have nothing to do with what we meet,
whether it is just or unjust."– Oswald Chambers*

Deep into the trek after the Serving King, an alarm will quietly begin
to rage deep within your being as you begin to notice an increasing lack
of 'justice' in the world around you. While a lack of justice in the life of
another will disturb you greatly at times, the quiet raging alarm will not
disable your trek after the Serving King, until that tragic moment, for life
is a tragedy, when 'justice' eludes you. It is in the moment of 'lost personal justice' that the trek may come to a sudden halt, for few of us are
well suited to a life without 'personal justice'.

Understand, it is not the total absence of justice in your life, but rather
those glaring moments when justice eludes your pursuit, ushering in a
hesitancy to continue the trek. You will be tempted to return to childhood
rants, "That's not fair," and refuse to move forward in your trek. And He
will respond to you from His station on the cross, "No, it is not." In that
moment, His challenge to disregard personal justice, rings forth, "deny
himself, take up his cross and follow Me" (Mark 8:34). It is this moment
of 'Gospel clarity' that devotion to the ways of God becomes crystal clear,
ushering in a new reality for those who trek after the Serving King, a
reality in which grace trumps justice, as Christ followers 'take up their
cross' and abandon claims for personal justice to reign.

Clearly, this is not a trek for the many, but for the few who 'take up
his cross'. This is not a call to be a Simon of Cyrene (Matthew 27:32)
carrying 'His cross'; to the contrary, it is the call to leave personal justice
behind and take up 'your cross'. 'Take up his cross' is the quintessence
of devotion to Christ. But be warned, 'justice' will not go 'quietly into the
night'; rather, the silent alarm will, more often than not, rage on deep
within you. Nonetheless, trek on as the alarm rages within.

Day 180
THIS CHANGES EVERYTHING

**Not that I have already obtained this or am already perfect,
but I press on to make it my own, because
Christ Jesus has made me His own.
(Philippians 3:12)**

"Never choose to be a worker; but when once God has put His call on you, woe be to you if you turn to the right hand or to the left. We are not here to work for God because we have chosen to do so, but because God has apprehended us."– Oswald Chambers

Early on in the trek after the Serving King, the trek will seem as a casual walk amongst friends who have arranged for their stroll through the park. However, a day is coming when the casual freedom shared between two friends begins to fade into the background, as a new reality begins to dawn, "Jesus has made me His own." This changes everything.

Paul, blinded in his Damascus encounter, released from his blurred religiosity, would spend the rest of his life as a 'slave' to Christ Jesus. What a glorious condition, this 'slavery' in Christ, in which you are told what you must do, "rise and enter the city and you will be told what you must do" (Acts 9:8). But when this Friend, Whom you have previously walked with in a leisurely manner, changes the nature of the stroll into the 'trek after the Serving King', you may chafe at His insistence; and insist He will.

It is in this moment of 'blinded opportunity' that life takes on the potential to be significant in ways no child of the King could have anticipated. But this significance, only seen by those who have been 'blinded', comes at a high price. 'Freedom', your cherished nemesis in life, your beloved 'freedom' that has led you down so many a wrong path, your most prized possession, must be surrendered to the Lordship of Christ. And "woe to you if you turn to the right hand or to the left."

Therein lies the crisis. 'Freedom' has been your closest friend. 'Freedom' even signed off on your stroll with Jesus. You and 'freedom' have journeyed countless miles together as you strolled through life together. Oh the 'close calls' the two of you have escaped as you ran through the chaos both of you have created. Now the temptation, in all of its power, rages in your being, as 'freedom' warns you over and over again not to let Jesus, "make you His own." This will change everything. Will you still "press on to make it my own?" Dare you trek on as His possession?

Day 181
THE NEW NORMAL

"And if your right hand causes you to sin, cut it off and throw it away. For it is better that you lose one of your members than that your whole body go into hell."
(Matthew 5:30)

"In the beginning Jesus Christ by His Spirit has to check you from doing a great many things that may be perfectly right for everyone else but not right for you. See that you do not use your limitations to criticize someone else."—Oswald Chambers

It is the "perfectly right for everyone else but not for you" that creates the rub for the child trekking after the Serving King. Such is the eventuality for those who intimately walk with Jesus as He begins to 'fine tune' you into His likeness. For indeed, it is the absence of the commonness of the 'right hand' which sets apart those who walk closest with Jesus, never content to bask in the 'forgiveness of sin', glorious as forgiveness is, but rather push on to the extreme of the 'eradication of sin'; but the extreme requires a willingness to step apart from the crowd of normality following after Jesus.

Breaking away from the 'normal' of the 'right-handed' crowd will rarely be easy, for they will find offense to your unconventional lack of 'right-handedness'. It creates an uncomfortableness for the crowd to have in their midst one who refuses to be 'normal'. They will prod you to simply bask in 'forgiveness of the right hand' like the rest of the 'right-handed' folks. You will be tempted in that moment to simply be normal, to keep the 'right hand' just like everyone else, to join the chorus of those singing praises to the forgiver of the 'right hand'. But Jesus has called you to a 'higher trek' leaving little room for the commonness of 'right-handed sin'.

This would be so much easier if Jesus had simply said, "And if your right hand causes you to sin, I will cut it off and throw it away." But He did not. Thus, the problem. It is you who must 'cut off' those common dimensions of life that have become detrimental to your trek after the Serving King, dimensions offending Him. Then the power of the metaphor becomes self-evident. It is the 'common' habits of the right hand, ways of being and doing, entertainments, etc., that must be 'cut off', if you are to join the ranks of those who have been liberated from the 'right hand'. Trek on, create and walk in the 'new normal' Jesus has called you to.

189

Day 182
THIS PRESENT OBEDIENCE

"Come to terms quickly with your accuser while you are going with him to court, lest your accuser hand you over to the judge, and the judge to the guard, and you be put in prison."
(Matthew 5:25)

"Jesus Christ is laying down this principle–Do what you know you must do, now, and do it quickly; if you do not, the inevitable process will begin to work and you will have to pay to the last farthing in pain and agony and distress."–Oswald Chambers

The trek after the Serving King takes on a new dimension for those fortunate enough to have been claimed by the King as His very own. Some, basking in the grace of forgiveness granted to all whom He claims, will assume a 'laissez-faire' approach to life, thinking life to be 'tariff' free, void of consequences for wrongs committed and obedience ignored. But nothing could be farther from the truth.

To the contrary, the standard of living for those claimed by the King rises to levels yet unseen for the child trekking after the Serving King. It is they who set the standard for integrity and consequence of behavior, good or bad. It is they who know the calling of the King and know His call ought to be carried out 'now', immediately in the present moment. And it is they, these 'claimed ones', who know consequences for rebellion against what "you know you must do," will 'inevitably' begin to unfold in the life of those trekking after the King. Expect these 'inevitable' consequences to work redemptively in remedying this 'present rebellion'.

However, never confuse the consequences of 'rebellion', swift and inevitable as they may be, with the consequences of simple failure. The two ought never to be confused. The latter, bathed in the grace of forgiveness, often tempered from the 'inevitable' consequence of 'falling short'. The former, rooted in rebellion, ushers in that 'inevitable process' and "you will have to pay to the last farthing in pain and agony and distress." Expect no 'free pass' when you have ignored what you 'must do'. Only the fool ignores what in the end must be done. Avoid the pain, agony and distress by simple obedience. Then the critical question arises, "What must I do as I trek on after the Serving King?" Trek on in this 'present obedience'.

EPILOGUE

———

The original conversation spanned an entire year, a full 366 days (including Leap Year), as Oswald and I swapped experiences over the kitchen table. The Publisher recommended a more manageable two-volume set of our dialogues; hence, the less cumbersome 182 pages. Nonetheless, if we have become friends and you would like to chat some more, please be sure to look for more conversations with Oswald and me in *More Mornings With Oswald* (expected publishing date Spring 2015).

I am currently writing a new devotional text, *Mornings in Romans*, available Fall 2015. Join me as I gather with a host of writers and thinkers from across the ages to collaborate on a dialogue with the Apostle Paul. Yep, expect another wild ride.

Trek on, dear friends! Trek on…

DON MINTER

Don and his wife, Laura, live in *Flagstaff, Arizona* where he serves as Lead Pastor for the Flagstaff Nazarene Church (FlagNaz). The Minters were delighted to return to Flagstaff after serving both Nazarene and Baptist churches in Oregon and South Carolina. If you are ever in Northern Arizona on a Sunday morning, please visit us at FlagNaz, 3505 E. Soliere Avenue, Flagstaff, AZ.

CPSIA information can be obtained
at www.ICGtesting.com
Printed in the USA
FFOW03n1041040417
34175FF